TIRED OF THINKING ABOUT DRINKING

TIRED OF THINKING ABOUT DRINKING

Take My 100-Day Sober Challenge

Belle Robertson

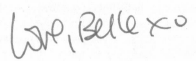

TOWER ROAD PRESS

TOWER ROAD PRESS
Saint John, NB Canada

Text Layout and Design: Belle Robertson, Tower Road Press
Fonts: Merriweather 10/16 for body; Knockout and DK
Visum for display headings. Do you need help formatting
your print or e-book? Shameless commercial link here:
www.towerroadpress.com

Cover Design: Kostis Pavlou

Printed and bound in Great Britain by Clays Ltd, Elcograf S.p.A.

First printing April 2016
Second printing May 2016
ISBN 978-0-9951580-0-9

Dedication

This book is for you.

This book is for my blog readers and my sober penpals. You are my sobriety insurance.

And this book is for all the non-joiners and lurkers. Yes, I can see you. I know you're out there.

And this book is for me. To say that quitting drinking changed my life would be a hilarious understatement.

Oh, and my husband.
He rocks.

CONTENTS

TIRED OF THINKING ABOUT DRINKING

INTRODUCTION

THIS IS WHAT I THOUGHT: There isn't enough to drink.

I should go to the liquor store now. I'm not sure what we have planned for tonight and I won't want to go out again. One bottle won't be enough. Two would be cutting it close. There isn't enough.

I will put our glasses side by side on the counter when I pour the wine each evening. I will line the glasses up to make sure that you don't get more. There isn't enough.

And this really happened to me. I was alone in a hotel room, and looked into the mini bar, and saw:

- one tiny Toblerone bar
- one KitKat bar
- one bottle of water
- two tiny cans of beer
- two tiny airplane-sized bottles of red wine

and I thought, I can't start drinking now, there isn't enough.

Not enough for what?

To fade out. To be numb.

Because despite what I may have said, I never wanted one glass of wine with dinner. I wanted three glasses. What's the point in one glass?

And despite what I may have said, I never drank because I liked the taste. I romanticized expensive wines, but they are all basically the same. Alcohol is a vehicle, and I didn't care which vehicle I used to travel. When the fancy stuff was gone, I was content to drink boxed white. I didn't let a room-temperature light beer stop me.

I didn't drink for the taste. I drank to get fuzzy. I wanted to be slightly numb, to take the edge off.

I spent a lot of time *taking the edge off* and then trying to maintain the edge taken off, but I usually ran into problems of sobering up too quickly, or drinking too much. There was no magic formula for edge-off-ness. I tried to find it. I tried having beer before wine, I tried eating first, I tried drinking on an empty stomach. There may have been a four-minute window of edge-off-ness and then I spent the rest of the night trying to find the four-minute window again. Mostly I found the couch, the remote, and pizza delivery.

THIS ISN'T YOU OF COURSE. Your story is completely different. You have a higher bottom than I do. Or a lower one. A 'bottom' in the sober world describes the point where you quit drinking. If you have a 'high bottom' then you quit when your problems were smaller. Poor concentration, missed deadlines, an inability to take advantage of new opportunities, procrastination, crappy sleep, many days of feeling ill. A 'low bottom' is where the micro problems have grown into larger holes, and might include health, relationship, money, or legal issues.

My high bottom looks like this: drink with dinner, and after, plan to drink less, continue to drink the same amount, try to quit for a month and manage nine days, start again, not keep my promises to myself. Wonder what the hell is wrong with me. Suffer with crappy sleep, extra pounds, wasted money.

That's my high bottom. (Don't I wish that I had not only a high drinking bottom, but also a TIGHT AND FIRM high bottom in real life. Alas.)

If alcohol is an elevator that only goes down, the goal is to step off, not to ride down any more. Stop drinking now. Start feeling better now.

I stepped off early. But I'm not naive. I know where that elevator was going. If I stopped 'before there was a problem' then I was fucking lucky, plain and simple. Because even stopping where I did, it was hard to do. Really hard.

Your bottom might look like falling down stairs, being sick, sleeping through fire alarms, days off work, drinking and driving, hiding recycling, bringing your own alcohol to events in case there isn't enough.

Your bottom might look like meetings or counsellors or doctors or medication. Your bottom could include rehab or outpatient treatment or jail.

I'm going to say something shitty now.

It doesn't matter *where* you are on the booze elevator. It's an elevator that only goes down. Quickly or slowly, but it is going down.

Here's another shitty thing while we're at it: It is hard to quit drinking no matter where you are on the elevator.

I only planned to stop drinking for 30 days, to 'take a break', and it was brutally hard, much harder than I thought it would be. I eventually looked online for help and found a diverse world of sober blogs. I read many. I started my own. And I found some comfort in shared stories of other high-bottom girls. I read advice from those further along in the sober world than I was. And I tried to take that advice.

So that's what this is, this thing you're holding in your hands, or that you're reading on your tablet, or that you're listening to in audio. This book thing is a (long) letter, from me to you, FROM someone who's been doing the sober thing for a while, TO someone who's considering the sober thing and doesn't (yet) know what to think. Or you're someone who IS sober, but aren't sure you like it, or aren't sure how to keep going. Or you've tried the sober thing before and now you're gathering some new ideas so that you can do it again.

Dear You,

I'm sending you a postcard from the sober future; I drank for a long time and have been sober for a few years. I can share my experience, which did turn out to be a pretty typical, early-sobriety experience, though to me it was freakishly challenging and unique.

In this letter to you, I can also give you a peek into the world of some of my sober penpals. I didn't mention the penpals yet? Ha. OK, here you go. I've had 2,400 sober penpals over the last three years. I know. Who does that?

I can honestly say, hand over heart, that I never intended to be sober, let alone to be a sober penpal with other wanting-to-be-sober-people. I never intended to write a blog, or to record over 100 episodes of a sober podcast, or to host sober meetups from London to Montreal, or to write a sober book.

Never.

I'm a girl who likes (liked) her wine.

And yet, I gave it up.

love, Belle xo

READ THIS: HOW TO NAVIGATE THIS BOOK.

You may be tempted to jump around and read from different sections in this book. My advice is that you read the text in order. The sections build on each other. If you turn directly to the challenge (Part 3) and you don't know the 'things you need to know' from Part 2, then it will seem too hard. It's easy to give up if you feel overwhelmed, so the writing is set up in a specific sequence. And based on the thousands of sober penpals that I've worked with so far, I do think it makes a difference *how* you learn this new way of thinking.

So you will start in the beginning, read straight through the four sections plus the Appendix. And then later you can dip back into the text and revisit specific places when you need to.

If you are still drinking, that's fine. Begin on page 1.

If you have already quit drinking and you have some sober momentum, that's fine too. Start in the beginning. There are ideas that will fill in as you read, like a photo developing. That makes it sound quite magical, doesn't it.

OK, so this text has four main sections. In Part 1, I'll tell you about me and my story. You'll see that you're not alone in this. In Part 2, I lay the foundation of things you will want to know about quitting drinking—both what it's like, and new ways to think about it. This is the 'things you need to know' section.

In Part 3, we'll look at the 100-Day Sober Challenge with more specifics (like how to do it!). There will be some places where I suggest that you send some emails to a general email inbox, to mark your different milestones. If you're anything like me, when you read self-helpy books, you probably have a tendency to skip the exercises. If you're like me, I always think: "I'm reading this book now, but I'm only skimming for ideas. I'm sort of half-in. Maybe I'll do the exercises later. Maybe not."

Instead, just for 100 days, just for the ideas contained in this book, just for now you can be all-in. Read the whole book, try all the sober things. Email when it says to email. Listen to the linked audio clips. Do the sober thing. Do the 100-Day Sober Challenge.

In Part 4, I want to share some of the personal emails I've received from sober penpals that address a lot of the same fears, concerns, worries, and joy that you may have. Yes, joy. It's waiting for you too. Really.

Finally, in the Appendix, I have a list of 60 sober tools, all the way from 'go to bed early' to 'inpatient rehab'. You will choose tools from the list to support you and to help make this sober thing easier.

Let's begin.

First, I'll tell you my story.

DISCLAIMER.

I know jack shit.

I'm a regular sober girl who hasn't had a drink in more than three years, mostly by accident. I originally planned to quit for Dry July, and was surprised to find it harder than I imagined. I was feeling really crappy at about day seven or eight, and in a 'fuck-it' moment, I started an anonymous online blog about being newly sober.

I had tried to stop drinking plenty of times on my own, but never managed to quit for more than a couple of days. Usually I'd declare my sobriety in the morning and then open a bottle of wine by 6 p.m. that same night. Then I'd quit again the next morning. One time I managed to go nine whole days without a drink. But I had no real support, no idea what I was doing, and I didn't know anyone who was happily sober. I knew someone with a low bottom who didn't drink anymore because of 'the incident', but I didn't know anybody like me, someone who was not an alcoholic but was (perhaps) going in that direction (soon) and who wanted to find a way to get things under control (assuming of course that that was possible) and having no idea how.

I tell you all of this because I want you to remember, when reading this book, that I am not a specialist of any kind. Really. I know jack shit. Please do not rely on a sober girl in a book for anything other than motivation or inspiration or humour. I am writing about me, about my experiences, and about the sober people I've been in contact with through my blog. Yes, the support that I used to quit drinking was entirely online, but let it be said (please) that some people *cannot* quit drinking without medical supervision. Please get professional help if you need it. If you don't have a doctor that you feel you can talk to, then find another doctor, or go to a walk-in clinic, or go to your hospital's emergency department and ask to speak to the psychiatrist on-call, or call a rehab facility's toll free number for advice. This book is not intended to be medical advice.

Now here's the official legal stuff:

This book will not make you thin or rich. Being sober is not the solution to all of life's problems. But it is a beginning.

MY ADVICE TO YOU.

I'm going to say some things in this book, and you will read them, and grumble, and you'll say to yourself: "Yes, I tried that already. It didn't work."

Or you'll say: "Belle, I know this specific thing you're recommending probably works for other people, but it won't work for me. I can tell before I even try."

So here's my advice. Just for the length of time it takes to read this book, try to imagine that what I'm saying here *does* work for you. Sometimes when we come up against new ideas, our first (natural) instinct is to think that it's not right for us.

A bit of an open mind will help. The way I write about being sober might be a new way of thinking for you. And maybe what you have tried before in terms of being sober hasn't been terribly successful for you. That's why you're here now. You're here to learn something different. You probably haven't tried being sober LIKE THIS before.

Be open to having your mind changed.

The sewer, the manhole cover, and the forecast is sunny

Quitting drinking is like getting out from underneath a manhole cover. It's a big, weighty thing that threatens to slam back down on us if we aren't careful.

When we're in the sewer (drinking) and we're covered by the manhole cover, well, we're dealing with a 'known' state. We know that the place smells, we know the view is terrible, that it's dark. There's no future. There is only regret and heartache.

When we get out of the sewer, and we stop drinking, at first we look over our shoulder, and we see the stinky sewer drinking hole. We let the manhole cover slam into place, and then we're standing alone in the sunlight. Quite terrified.

We try to explain the sewer and the manhole cover and the desperation to normal drinkers, and they don't really understand. We slowly, block by block, day by day, begin to walk AWAY from the hole behind us. With or without sober tools, with or without support. With or without knowing what the fuck we're doing.

And now there are two choices. We can continue to look behind us. See the hole again and again. Periodically test how heavy the manhole cover is. Sample the delicious aroma of the sewer. Or we can walk forward, into a place unknown, where it is forecast to be sunny with cloudy periods.

Yes. Bad crap still happens in the sunny place (kids, job, money, health), and yes, you might be tempted to turn around and look longingly at the sewer. You'll think that maybe it'd be a good idea to go back there, just for a minute, because at least it's dark and quiet and stinky and depressing in there . . .

But my darling, let me say this: Booze isn't a *solution* to a problem. It's a very temporary pause button (manhole cover) with horrendous consequences. It'd be like turning to heroin. It isn't the right solution for the problem.

You might need time off, help, someone to talk to, a break, to cry, to yell, to vent, to write, to run, to sleep. You may not know yet what you need to do to feel better. But with 100% certainty, slamming your hand in the manhole cover (drinking) isn't a solution. I agree you need some solutions. You don't need to add problems. Let's find you a solution.

~~~~~

Source: Blog post, www.100daysoberchallenge.com/thesewer

PART I. ABOUT ME

IT STARTS AT 3 A.M., WAKE UP, ROLL OVER, not too quickly or the nausea will start. Try to be still, flat on your back. Hot. Thirsty. Headache. Take a small sip of water as a trial, to see how it goes. Not well. Guilt. It happened again. Angry words. Crying. Shift in the bed again. Why is it so hot in here. Then cold. One foot out from under the blanket—oh it's no use, the room has started to move.

I never want to do this again. I never want to wake up in the middle of the night both wishing I was dead and hoping I'm not dying. Let me not vomit tonight, please, and I promise I will cut back on the drinking. I never want to feel this bad, at this hour of the night, feel so hopeless, alone, scared, dark.

I am definitely drinking too much. I should face that. I should stop drinking for a week, take a break. I'll start tomorrow. After the work party. After vacation. Next week. After the birthday. The first of the month. On a Monday.

I promise.

And when we do eventually fall asleep, there is some relief. Sleep is a break. It is swiftly followed by a too-bright morning, a new beginning, a chance to start again. For real this time.

You get up and go for a run, have a healthy breakfast. You drink water. You meditate. You quickly do an online search for "do I need to stop drinking" but don't find an answer.

Anyway, last night—THAT won't happen again. Next time I'll eat first, alternate with water, stop after two glasses of wine, I won't order pizza at 11 p.m., I won't go home with a stranger, wake up outside, fall down the stairs, or drunk-text my ex. I won't do that again.

Next time it'll be fine.

I'll have one glass with dinner like people do on television. Or maybe I'll take a break from drinking for a few months. That should be easy enough. If I can quit for a bit then it's probably not a problem. Anyway, the online questionnaire said that if I'm not drinking in the morning then I might not be an alcoholic.

Because only alcoholics benefit from quitting drinking. No one else would quit, would they? To sleep better, spend less money, lose weight, and feel proud of themselves? No one just stops drinking alcohol, do they? What about the missing out, the fun, what about celebrations, and boredom? What about all those hypothetical wine tours in Italy? What would I say to people? How would I explain?

The sweaty night turns into a bright morning. The promise to have a few sober days cycles around again. The afternoon turns into an anxious waiting for time to pass. There is a certainty that something needs to change. But today is not the day to begin. And the bottle of wine opens at 6:00 p.m. We begin again.

I TRIED TO QUIT DRINKING, failed, tried again, got some momentum, and then things started to improve. A lot. I am now more than three and a half years without a drink, and I can assure you that I never intended to do this. It's like an accident: I tripped, fell, and got sober. As it turns out, I *like* being sober more than I like drinking. Who knew.

My drinking story, such as it is, lacks the dramatic lows and spectacular crashes you have seen in movies. There is an absence of sleeping under bridges. There aren't any bottles hidden in brown paper bags. I never woke up in a strange city.

I'm not sure why my story is as 'good' and 'high-bottomed' as it is. Don't get me wrong, I'm relieved, because I had many intersections with alcohol that could have introduced a shit-ton of crappiness (which is the direct opposite of 'happiness'). Bad intersections with alcohol include: Fall and tear a hole in the knee of my jeans. Oh well, now they're trendy. Nearly passing out in the bathtub. I'm tired and this bath is nice and warm and I'll finish this wine, oh maybe I'll close my eyes for a minute I'm so exhausted—wait, sleeping in the tub is probably a bad idea. Maybe it's dangerous, I'm not sure. OK, I'll finish this wine and then get out of the tub. And the driving. Surely I can have two glasses of wine and then drive. I could probably have three, it's not that far. I'll go straight home, there won't be much traffic.

Yes, I know.

If you knew me when I was drinking, you are reading this now and thinking: "What the fuck is this? YOU certainly didn't have a drinking problem. YOU didn't get drunk every night. YOU weren't stumbling home from the pub after having spent $200 on fish and chips and drunkenly buying rounds for everyone. YOU weren't a fall-down drunk. Lots of people drink more than you ever did."

This is all true.

I owned two companies. I dealt with clients. I met dead-lines, ran, went to school, graduated, learned to speak French, self-published cookbooks for my family for Christmas.

And I liked alcohol. Shrug. Maybe not more than other people. But I liked it. And alcohol liked me.

[As an aside, shall we talk about Christmas? Yes, we shall. Why not now, at the beginning of this recollection of things. Remember the year I got a bottle of Scotch as a gift? I hated the taste, but couldn't waste perfectly good alcohol, and as long as it was in the house, it was calling out "Drink Me" every evening. So I mixed glasses of scotch with ginger ale and orange juice, to finish it off, until the bottle was empty. If alcohol was in the house, it spoke to me, then I drank it. Even if I didn't really enjoy it.

But let's be fair. I finished bottles not just at Christmas. Every single thing I did had an association with alcohol. Celebrations, gallery openings, tree trimmings, vacations, graduations, weddings, New Year's, funerals. (Deep breath.) I associated drinking with grief and happiness, with disappointment and elation. With snowstorms and beaches. Any reason was a good reason to drink. Brunch? Drink earlier.]

IF YOU TRY TO GO BACK TO THE BEGINNING, and you look at me when I'm 20 years old, my alcohol consumption is—at that time—quite tiny. Can you see me there with the tall 1980s hair? I am working full-time at my first real job that includes ironed clothes and nylons, and I buy a six-pack of cider and consume exactly one bottle each night to 'unwind'. That's what adults do. They unwind. If invited out for drinks and everyone around me was doing shots, I stuck to my one bottle of cider.

Even then, I had a voice in my head that said "Drink. Drink Now." It didn't seem particularly worrying to me when I admitted to friends that alcohol spoke to me. I smiled and explained my rules: I only ever have one drink and that I didn't keep extra alcohol in the house. I thought I was very clever. I'd grown up around plenty of booze. It wasn't pretty. So me, taking care of me, I was vigilant.

I had no idea then that normal drinkers didn't think about alcohol at all, and explaining that 'alcohol speaks to me' made me look like a wacko. How could I possibly have known, since I am not one, that normal drinkers measure their alcohol consumption like I measure my corn on the cob consumption—which is to say, not at all.

Just like I have days without corn, normal drinkers have plenty of days without alcohol but they're not keeping track. I don't pay attention to whether you are getting more corn than me, and a normal drinker fills up glasses around her without worrying about who's getting how much. And yes, it's true that corn on the cob is my favourite of all summer things to eat, but I have never planned days around when I can eat it. I have never gone out at 11 p.m. to get more corn. I've never worried about running out of corn.

Sorry. I know this next part will seem shitty and unfair, but you're reading this so I have to ask you: Do you know the exact last date when you ate a perfect cob of yellow corn? (For me, I was on vacation, it was about 8 or 9 or 10 weeks ago, not sure.)

Now tell me, when did you last have a drink? You remember.

I remember the date of my last drink, it was June 30th, 2012. And I didn't even like it.

UNLIKE CORN ON THE COB, which I always enjoy and never binge on, my last drink was something that I forced down.

I was quitting drinking as an experiment called Dry July. And for those last few days in June, before my forced Day 1 sober, I drank every night. Not because I felt like it, but because it was the allocated end-of-drinking time in preparation for a month off. I wasn't even interested in the wine at that point. *I was drinking because it was the thing I did.* No enjoyment. No taste. No feeling except for exhaustion. Like a hammer banging on my head.

How did I get from one drink a day in my 20s, all the way to doing a Dry July some 25 years later? Shall I say "One drink at a time"? That's not very funny, but it is true.

If alcohol is an elevator that only goes down, then I was on a slow descent. So slow, that I didn't notice. I had lots of drinking rules and guidelines for myself, and over time, bit by bit, I broke all of my rules. I know that will sound familiar to you.

"You'll violate your standards quicker than you will lower them" (said the genius, Robin Williams, as a sober guy).

There is a barely visible but certain turning point where shit starts to get weird in my story. If you roll the tape forward from age 20 to where I am 34 years old, you can see me dating Mr. Trainwreck. I think everyone has at least one of these "not good from the beginning" relationships. We had nice romantic picnics on the living room floor with all things French and exotic (baguettes and paté are exotic when you live in a medium-sized city in English Canada). Most nights we split a six-pack of beer.

After a five month relationship—that had more than its share of chaotic emotions, sex, charm, music, compulsive lying, fighting, door slamming, crying, and making up—he left me, never called again, just turned and walked away.

Dating this guy was lovely and grim rolled into one package. I was shocked when he disappeared, but also relieved that it was over. Yes, there was therapy. To figure out what seemed attractive about this guy, and to ensure that I never had a relationship like that again. (The therapy must have worked. I haven't.)

But once Mr. Trainwreck left, I continued to buy six-packs of beer, some nights drinking four bottles myself. To be sensible, though, to continue my "alcohol speaks to me so I am vigilant" façade, I would always line up the beer caps on the counter so that I didn't lose count and accidentally over-drink.

This is the beginning of me drinking too often. There is no big dramatic event. It isn't post-partum depression, or the death of a parent, or the loss of a job that tipped me into daily drinking. It was a stinky, shitty, lying, charismatic boyfriend, who finally left me because I was too insecure to leave him first.

I started drinking most nights. I taped movies so that I would always have something to watch. My after-work routine was TV, beer, cigarettes, and me on the couch rolled up in a blanket like a burrito. It was always a dark room. I'd have a few drinks and get that TV-zen-feeling. Some nights I made dinner. Some nights I had roast potatoes and left the rest of the expensive groceries untouched in the fridge. Some nights I had popcorn for dinner. Many nights. Most.

I did variations of this, more or less, for years. My journal for this post-crazy-boyfriend time says things like "I drink differently from other people. I'm only going to drink on special occasions or when socializing. Only on weekends."

But of course, you and I both know that only drinking on weekends is tricky. Because what about Sunday night? Is Sunday part of the weekend? What about Thursday? Maybe the weekend is four days long. Maybe it is, in fact, most of the week.

I clung, for a very very very very long time, to this idea of having rules, and I kept adjusting them, trying to find some guidelines that I could actually follow. I was sure there must be some trick that I'd yet to find, that would let me handle my consumption and therefore not have to quit entirely.

In order to develop what I thought of as my alcohol self-control-muscles, I did many short sober stints, to prove to myself that everything was fine. No wine for one day. For two days.

Then the voice would start.

Is it time yet? You can drink now. Celebrate sobriety with a glass or two. You've done well. You are going to break this non-drinking stretch anyway, so you might as well drink now. Drink tonight and quit later. What about now.

Is it time to drink yet? Where is that waiter. Can I get another one. Will they notice if I refill my glass from this bottle.

Is it too soon to order another round. I don't want this evening to end, I want this party to go on and on.

Wait, are you going home now? You're no fun.

I'll finish up this bottle before I go to bed. I'll bring the last glass of wine into the bedroom with me, put it on the bedside table, and sip until I close my eyes.

I would sometimes extend a two-day sober break to be three or four or five days. Then things got strange, the drinking noise in my head louder, more insistent.

You are a fuck up, you're single, you've got nothing. You might as well drink. What else can you do alone in the evenings. Pop a tape in the VCR, watch "Big" or "Terms of Endearment" or "Tootsie"?

Have a few beers, some wine. You're boring. You can't read every night.

I keep you company. I can fill the spaces.

I am your best friend. I am always there when you need me.

The "Drink Now" voice, which I call Wolfie, will say *anything* to get us to drink. Nothing is off-limits. Wolfie hits below the belt. Wolfie talks smack.

from FacingMeNow:
"Wolfie with a megaphone said to me: You've had a long, crazy day. Have a drink. You'll just have one. It will take the edge off. You have blown this whole thing out of proportion. You need to cut back, not quit. A hundred fucking days? You'll never make it anyway. You're not going to drink because you told a woman you've never met, who lives halfway across the world, that you wouldn't?"

WHEN I AM 39 YEARS OLD, I get married for the first—and so far the only—time. Completely different guy from Mr. Train-wreck boyfriend. Mr. Belle is lovely, good company, even-tempered, reliable, and he doesn't even tell white lies.

Once married, you may predict that my drinking-because-lonely feelings would evaporate, and that my evenings of time-filling, booze-is-my-best-friend-drinking would end.

And while the gaping loneliness *did* end, the new gift that marriage provided me was a perfect partner in crime. I'd open a bottle, he'd finish it. We'd drain the last bit of wine late on a Sunday evening and there'd be only one place open at that hour and it's snowing? No worries, he'll go out while I wait at home revelling in how lucky I am to have married so well.

[To avoid these snowy late-night trips, did you ever try buying a case of wine, thinking that if it was around all the time you'd feel less compulsive about it, and drink less?

Ha. Really. Who was I kidding? With a case of wine in the house, I drank more. Of course I did. We never had a wine collection or a wine rack or a wine cellar or a liquor cabinet either. Alcohol didn't last long enough to be collected or displayed or shared.]

With my husband-drinking-partner-in-crime we played house like grown-up real people, and we had wine with dinner. We opened five bottles at a time and had a 'pinot noir taste test'. We made deals as a couple to skip one day each week, no booze. I didn't buy any wine that day. Instead there was probably mid-afternoon beer. Or a port before bed. But no wine.

WE MOVED TO EUROPE, THE LAND OF CHEAP WINE. I taught a self-discipline class (insert hilarious laugh track here), and while my students set goals of "eat no bread for two days" or "work on new business plan two days in a row"—my goal was usually "no alcohol for two days."

And I *could* do it. I could quit drinking for two days. It's a lot like holding your breath and going underwater. It requires focus, elimination, and tunnel vision. I couldn't go outside. I certainly didn't go for groceries because there was a wine store in the same shopping complex. I felt moderately stable until something happened, like if I got frustrated, or mad, or sad, or bored, or if something good happened and I had to celebrate.

I had completely maladaptive coping strategies (which I talk about more in Section 10: Avoid 'Overwhelm'). And in quitting for such short periods of time—the longest was nine days—I never had any of the benefits of being sober. I didn't learn any coping strategies. I avoided everything, waiting waiting waiting until I could drink again.

If you'd have suggested that I quit for longer, so that I could get used to being sober, I would have laughed in your face for half an hour. *Are you kidding me? I am a girl who likes her wine. That's who I am. I don't have a problem. I'm not like those people.*

IT WAS A SHITTY PLACE TO END UP. I knew I drank more than I wanted to, but I was *certain* I wasn't an alcoholic. I knew that something had to change, but I was certain that being 100% sober was unachievable and unrealistic long-term. And completely undesirable. I knew I had a very loud Wolfie "Drink Now" voice in my head that insisted that a glass of wine with dinner was normal. I also knew that there was another very quiet, very tiny mouse-like voice, that said: You have to stop. You know what this internal conflict is like.

I didn't drink and fall down. I didn't black out. I didn't lose my job. (If you're still drinking, you're supposed to say 'yet' after phrases like that: *I haven't lost my job yet.*)

My biggest problem was the *thinking*. The incessant thinking about drinking. Honestly, it was so time consuming. How, when, where, how much, did he have more than me, will there be enough, is there time to go out to buy more.

And while the noise in my head was very large, and very tiring, my problem didn't seem real. Over-thinking about over-drinking seemed like such a small thing compared to the alcohol-fuelled dramas in movies. I mean, everything we know about drinking and addiction and alcoholism we know from television and it's filtered through AA. On TV programs, people are in recovery, going to meetings, but we know that this is a setup for them to relapse later in the season (with dramatic car crash results). We're presented with the idea that all drunks relapse.

No one on television is sober and living happily ever after. If you think about it—and I did—there isn't a television program where someone looks like me. No one on television ever complains of being tired of thinking about drinking. No one goes go online, searches for "do I need to stop drinking" or "help for sobriety without AA." Which is what I did. Then I'd open some more wine, watch A&E's "Intervention," about drug and alcohol abuse, people being taken to rehab, mostly ambushed and coerced into treatment by their families and psychologists. I'd watch this show and cry.

I even wrote a message to myself, late at night, near the bottom of a bottle of wine, hoping I would read it the next morning and that it would mean something.

this is my code for "turn the page"

It gets between me and my life,

between me and you, between me and serving, between me and fun. It affects my weight, my sleep, my enthusiasm. It blunts, fills, numbs, fills time, expands into the space allowed. Adds nothing, feels bad, sad, argumentative, irritated. Isn't the real me. There's nothing to escape from, it isn't bad here, there's joy and beauty and ease here. Don't need to 'go' anywhere else.

~~~~~~

Source: Handwritten note from tipsy-me to sober-morning-me, Autumn 2011, about 10 months before I quit.

THEN A FRIEND EMAILED ME, and complained about how hard being sober was for him. He started a private blog and invited me and one another male friend to join. In this blog, behind closed doors, our plan was to talk openly about quitting drinking.

I'm quitting drinking for a month.

I am not an alcoholic. I grew up with booze around me though, in its very nasty, woe-is-me, depressed shadow. By contrast, I'm very vigilant (too vigilant) about how much I drink, and when. I've come to a point where 'thinking' about drinking is taking up too much of my time. Planning when I can have a drink (6 p.m.), counting how many I have (let's stop at 1, how about 2, never more than 3). I'm tired of sleeping poorly. I'm tired of watching the clock to see how long it is until 6 p.m.

I drink green tea and herbal tea all day anyway, and now that I've quit I just continue with the tea after dinner. I realize that the noise in my head is going—the bargaining—the voice that was always asking "Can I have some wine?" It's so much quieter in my head now. Anyone else feeling more quiet without alcohol?

I do think that life without alcohol is boring though. I'm surprised at how much time I could fill with three glasses of wine (an entire evening!). I often find myself gaping at the wide abyss that begins at 6:30 p.m., and I actually find myself saying "Yes, but NOW what will I DO?" Which is quite hilarious, considering I'm in charge of my two tiny businesses, I help my husband with his newly self-employed life, and I'm running a catering company out of my apartment. It's not like I don't have stuff to do.

What's working so far is having daily projects. Last night, instead of three glasses of wine, I worked on a new recipe for chocolate espresso cupcakes with frosting. I did a trial of taking pictures of the cupcakes with an entirely white background using diffused light (worked beautifully). I had a bath and read in the tubbie. I went to bed at 10:30 p.m. and read some more.

At first I thought I would give up wine for a month, to prove that I could, but in reading my blog entries here straight through, I'm now wondering if in fact I'm giving it up forever.

Not because it's creating problems in my life, not because I'm out of control.

But because my life has so much MORE good stuff in it when the wine is gone. More sleep, more reading, more projects, fewer calories, less crankiness, less noise.

And as a good Canadian girl, I must now quote The Tragically Hip: "I'm tired of thinking 'bout drinking . . ."

Double Chocolate
Cupcake with
Mocha Swiss
Buttercream Frosting

Source: Blog post from now-deleted private blog, mid-April 2012, two and a half months before I quit.

When I read that now, I'm shocked at how well-formed my ideas are. I had the name of my future blog. And I knew why I wanted to quit.

I can also see that I had my carefully-considered rationalizations in place. I made sure they knew that *I wasn't an alcoholic*. I wrote that in April. I'm not sure how long I'd been sober at that point, maybe only a few days, but my plan was to quit for a month to prove that I could. Because if you can quit for a while, you don't have a problem, right?

I guess I was *practising* being sober. I thought blogging with those two guys would be helpful. It wasn't. Except—to be kind—it's true that I have always used writing as a way to explain things to myself, and this was me beginning to explore my drinking through writing. The idea that anyone (later) would find my writing to myself (on my public blog) to be "honest, transparent, raw, inspiring, gritty, transformative" would have been hilarious in the extreme. I can assure you that when you're trying to quit drinking, and you're writing your shit on your blog or elsewhere, you're doing it for NO other reason than to try to make sense of it for yourself. The thought of an audience would have been chilling (they'll recognize me, I have nothing to say, I'm so lost here I can't be an example to anyone for anything, don't look at me too closely I'm about to relapse, please don't watch).

WHEN I DISCOVERED THE SOBRIETY BLOG 'Unpickled', I had a *holy-shit* response. Are there other people who have done this sober thing that I'm trying to do, who have been successful, who live happily ever after without booze?

That first sober blog represented, at the very least, the existence of ONE other person on the planet who felt (like I did) that she drank more than she wanted to, that she found it hard to moderate, and that she had decided to quit alcohol entirely, and was all the happier for it.

Before I found 'Unpickled', I had no idea that sober blogs existed. I know, it seems like a 'duh' moment now. I *had* searched online for questionnaires like "do I need to quit drinking" or "am I an alcoholic" but I had never searched for "does anyone quit drinking who isn't an alcoholic?" I could have saved myself a lot of time.

That shitty Wolfie voice in my head had me convinced that I was broken. I resigned myself to the fact that there was only AA and the whole stereotype of sitting in a room, showing your face, recounting your horrors, being supported by drinkers with low bottoms—I didn't want it. I know now that AA helps a shit ton of people. Thousands and millions. But when it was me and Wolfie, alone in my head, I knew that I was not going to go to AA. Because I didn't have *that kind of problem*.

I know I'm not alone. I get emails all the time that say "I might drink myself to death. I can't go to AA."

When I read 'Unpickled', a blog written by a woman who sounded like me, I finally thought: "Here's an idea that might work for me."

..

DRY JULY IS A CANCER FUNDRAISER IN AUSTRALIA. When I learned about the 30-day sober challenge, it felt like a good idea. The plan for Dry July is you join a bunch of people, strangers, and everyone quits drinking for a fixed length of time.

I figured July 1st would be a perfect time to do my month-off-drinking-to-prove-I-don't-have-a-problem. I'd start on the first of the month thanks to the magical thinking that says there's a right day, a right way, a right time, the right alignment, the perfect moment, the moon phase, the stars, the angels dancing on a pin just for me. Also being a good Canadian, July 1st is Canada Day. *Oh Canada*. Go me.

I told you that my last drink was choked down on June 30th. I haven't told you about that month leading up to Dry July. For all of June that year, I was travelling: seven flights, international and domestic, from Europe to North America, to see family, friends, and husband's family. It was a continuous stream of rental cars, temporary apartments, meals out, visits with old friends, and seeing some people for the first time in five years.

There was alcohol. At every opportunity, every meal, every gathering. *She's in town let's go for lunch, have some wine. Dinner. Come by our place first for drinks. Let's drink like old times. It's so good to see you, I don't have any friends here who've known me as long as you have, can we meet again while you're here—we can get wine.*

And drink. I did.

For that whole month while travelling, I woke late, ate crappy cereal, spoke with Europe before they went to bed.

I ran half-heartedly in the city where I'd completed my one and only marathon.

Not only did I not repeat my glorious long training runs along the seawall with the mountains and the ocean, there was only ONE single night in that entire month-long vacation where I didn't drink. And that's the night I nearly died.

A high school graduation party, one of the grand-parents in attendance was 'sober' and so the family didn't have any alcohol at the event out of respect for him. So we didn't drink and I left at midnight and was driving home to the rental place way the fuck across the city over a bridge, and across another city.

I'm on the bridge, and although I used to live here, I've been gone for ten years, and I can't remember which exit to take off the bridge, and then I promptly go too far, and take the wrong exit. Now I'm in the middle of highway construction, the kind where the roads are slick with newly tarred asphalt, there are trucks and rollers and barriers. There are on-ramps and off-ramps but they're skinny and badly painted, temporary lines, go this way for now, then later you can go that way.

I come off the bridge, in the wrong place, so I have to waste time doing the loop-de-loop of the ramps to get turned around. I finally come down the hill where I can re-enter the highway, going back the right way.

The merging on-ramp lane to the highway would usually be long and well-marked. You'd come down a hill and have some time, minutes even, to drive parallel with the road so that you could check your mirrors before merging into a highway that's going 100 km per hour (60 mph).

Not this on-ramp. Not this time.

Around the bend, down the hill, I headed to the merge lane and then the newly painted lane stops abruptly at the highway. I slam on the brakes, my car does not travel even one inch beyond where it's supposed to, I'm within the painted lines but only just. I turn my head to check for oncoming traffic (how many times had I rolled through that kind of intersection, checking only after I was in the lane. How many times had I been drinking—even one glass—and had to navigate something as awful, disorienting, tiring, black and confusing as a construction site at midnight).

I turn my head to check, and then—right then—not a second to spare, literally not one second, a huge blasting 18-wheeler truck comes tearing past me, near enough to spit on, the draft of its proximity sucking and then blowing my rental car. The amount of space between me and being flattened? Inches. The amount of time between when I stopped my car and when the truck roared by? Not one second. Not even. It was simultaneous.

The truck goes by. I sit there for a long moment. I'm shaking. Adrenaline. Near death fear. Craning my neck now to see anything coming from anywhere. I cautiously drive back to the rental apartment. In bed that night, I wake every two hours, replaying the hill-brake-swoosh of the truck. This wasn't a 'near miss story' you tell friends at the pub, with embellishments and hilarious exaggerations.

This was a 'near miss reality', of inches, seconds, large truck, girl in small rental car, being killed on vacation.

And the girl was completely sober.

Every time I'd wake up and think of the wind-suck-roar of the truck—I knew. If I'd been drinking, even one glass, I'd be dead.

This wasn't me trying to tell a good story. This is dead. Really dead. The kind of dead where the car is pulled under the axle of the truck and dragged screeching for half a mile down the road before the driver of the truck can come to a stop. That kind of dead.

Badly marked highway in a construction zone? Yes. Off-ramp not marked with an appropriate speed limit? Yes. Sign to indicate a T-intersection instead of merging on-ramp was missing? Yes. Girl sober so that she could respond appropriately and even then only barely make it through? Yes. Girl going to keep drinking after that? Surely not.

And yet.

I REMEMBER MY DAY ZERO, the last day of drinking. It wasn't even very celebratory. You know how you picture your final hurrah will be something shiny and bright? Instead, I was draped across the fold-up bed/couch thing in the home office, watching an episode of "Top Chef" on the computer screen. I was on my second glass of wine. Maybe third. It didn't taste like anything. I didn't feel warm and buzzy. I was drinking because it was my last night, not because there was anything appealing about it. It was anaesthesia.

The room got smaller, the edges got darker, me and the TV show. Nothing to do. Nothing to feel. No real excitement. Except when something happened on the cooking show and I came out of the office and said to my husband, "I think I'll go to culinary school and be a chef."

Which translates to: "I want some of the excitement that they are apparently having on that show to be in MY life, too. How can I get that into my life? Oh, you mean disconnect this booze anaesthesia from my arm? I don't think it is related. I'm pretty sure that booze only numbs the bad parts of my life. It can't be numbing the good too, can it?"

ALL OF THE DAY ZEROS ARE HARDER THAN A DAY 1. At least on Day 1 you are underway. Things have the possibility of improving, of you feeling better. When you're still over-drinking and wishing you weren't, you can read sober blogs, see people on the other side of the sober glass and wish you were there. It's too easy to feel angry at the happy sober people because they have something you don't. Then the booze voice in your head tells you that maybe those sober people are exaggerating how good it is, I mean how good can it feel to be sober? Can it be as good as "freshly shaved legs in a bed with clean sheets."

It does sound culty, doesn't it? All the sappy sentiments: "Quit drinking and your life will be magical, it's like fresh bread and big hugs and thick blankets and starry nights."

Because when it was me thinking about quitting drinking, all I could see going forward was days and days of shit.

Potential withdrawal, sleeplessness, terrified of how I'd explain why I wasn't drinking. How would I go on vacation, celebrate, or have sex sober? How would I go to Napa in ten years on some magical wine tour that I've always planned but had never done? What about my brother's wedding. If I can't have expensive champagne in my glass, then the event will be ruined and I'll hate my life. "Those sober people are faking, fucked up, false. Sobriety is not that good, it's shit, I'm shit, being sober is shit, let's have a beer."

So if Day 0 is the shittiest of days—still drinking, wishing you weren't, following sober people online, wanting what they have—then what's the best day? There are many. Let's start with an obvious one. Day 1 is a very good day. It's the day that things are finally underway, it's the day you decide that this shit has to change. You don't know what to expect. You know that parts are going to be gigantically crappy. But you know that you can't live on Day 0 anymore.

When I woke up on Day 1, it was mostly uneventful. I read a sober blog, went for a run, ate some cereal, did the laundry, and I said to myself: "Today's the day. There are parts of this early sober thing that are going to be rotten. But today is a beginning. Onwards."

Dear You: As I write this part now, I'm between a rock and a hard place. If I say that the first week sucked rocks— if you hear that it was hard—then you are not going to want to do it. If I tell you it was all sunshine and roses, you won't believe that either.

Instead, I'll tell you what happened to me. I was pretty psyched for the first few days. I was proud of myself. I had distractions, events planned for the evenings (and when I say 'event' I mean I had cupcakes to bake). I had a replacement drink. I read sober blogs. I maybe didn't sleep totally well, but it wasn't disastrous. I maybe had a headache (dehydration) so I drank more coffee. I liked coffee when I was drinking, but once sober—now—I love coffee. A lot. It tastes better or something.

For the first week, I was doing what I'd always done before. I was *trying harder*. Sort of like holding my breath, waiting for it to feel better. Try harder, try harder.

Then on the evening of Day 7, the sober shit hit the gigantic fan and I had a terrible day that stretched into evening. I couldn't face making dinner. My replacement drink was unappealing. My husband didn't know anything about what I was trying to do, or why I was so cranky. I was mad at the world that I was trying to be sober and frustrated that it was so fucking hard.

Let's sit right here for a second feeling antsy, twitchy, and irritated. This is the place where the decision gets made. *I want to drink, I want to be sober, I can't figure out what to do. The noise in my head is very loud, I can't see any options.* Drinking seems like the only solution—the one thing that I know will take away this crappy feeling. I don't have the skills to try anything else to feel better because—duh—I've been using wine as my only coping mechanism. I've overused wine as a feel-better tool for so long that I literally cannot remember one single thing I could do instead to ease my mood.

Imagine PMS on a long haul flight and you're hungry. It's "oh my god what can I do here, I have to do something, nothing is going to work, I'm out of ideas, there's no solution, I can't do this, it's too hard, what am I doing anyway, I could solve this terrible feeling if I had a drink. But if I drink it creates a new set of problems, so now I Literally Have Nothing to help me feel better. There's nothing. The world is a gaping void of things that won't help."

I rapidly flick through some rolodex of choices, finding all of them to be unsatisfactory. None will work fast enough. I know I don't want to drink, but I don't know much else. I look at the rolodex of diversions, of tools. Fuck it, I'll try some of these things—but they won't work—I can already tell.

Let's start with a bath at supper time. The crazy wolf brain is yelling 'wine wine wine wine' and I start to fill the tub.

The brain says: *It's not tub time now, this is delaying the inevitable, you know you're going to drink.*

I add bubble bath that smells like cedar. How clever. Who invents this stuff? It's in a nice masculine blue bottle. Nothing pink or frilly about this. It's anti-Wolfie bubble bath. I'm sure of it.

This won't work, I can yell for a long time here.

I sit in the tub until I'm pruney. I read, then fret, then read again, then plan to change the world, then read some more. Dip my hair into the bath water. I'm going to wait here until I feel better. Lie back and try to float in the small tub. I'm going to get up and get dressed and have wine.

Turn and face the other way, faucet at my back. This is ridiculous, I feel terrible, this can't be normal, this can't be healthy. Turn and sit sideways. I'm itchy in my own skin. I don't want to drink but I can't figure out what else I'm supposed to do. Add more hot water. There must be a comfortable position but I can't find it. Fuck it, I'm going to drink, this is ridiculous. I've already quit for a week. Let's celebrate sobriety with some alcohol.

I get out of the tub, dry off, put on one of my husband's heavy metal t-shirts, inside-out so that the tag doesn't scratch me (I try not to cut the tags out of his shirts, only my own). I wear red plaid pyjama bottoms with a draw-string and pockets. The orange Ernie socks. Wet hair up in a pony tail.

I sit in front of the laptop. I read the webpage that is sitting open. Some anonymous woman going through her own journey without alcohol, a sober blog.

It inspires me. Her words are enough.

I get up, make myself a special drink of black currant syrup, Perrier, grapefruit juice.

No, no, you don't want to have that now, it's much better if you drink wine on an empty stomach, you're ruining things, don't do it, shit, I don't fucking want juice.

Husband is looking at me. He doesn't know what state I'm in (or why). I'm not making dinner, I say.

But you always make dinner and drink while you cook. If you let him cook, he'll ruin it and the kitchen will be a mess and it's better if you do it yourself. Then you can drink in the kitchen where he can't see what you're doing, and you can drink from his glass before you hand it to him, and you can make sure you get enough.

I take my special bitter grapefruit drink and sit in the living room, big floor-to-ceiling windows. It's a warm July evening and there will be light in the sky until 10:30 p.m. I'm facing the courtyard, trees, lots of birds here in Europe that we didn't have back home. New sounds.

I'll start up again tomorrow night, you know. This might be over for tonight, but I haven't gone away. I'll come back and torture you again. This whole bath, special drink, not making dinner, looking outside thing—it'll get old. I'll be back. You need me.

I sip the drink, I can hear the husband banging around with the pots so that he can make roast potatoes and sausages (a dinner he can make without asking questions, as he senses—rightly so—that speaking to me right now will not go over well). I listen to the unidentifiable birds. Across the courtyard the teenager practises his saxophone. The family downstairs has a screamy child. The granny likes to lean over her window railing with the phone in her hand, talking to someone I can't see, about something I can't understand, in a language I don't speak. She pulls her pink button-up cardigan around her. Always the same cardigan, grey skirt, white blouse. Every day.

I sip the drink again. I reach up to rebundle my wet hair into the elastic. It's nice here. The witching hours are over for tonight.

..

THE NEXT MORNING, I know that things have to change. I can't keep trying 'harder'. I have to do something 'different'. Oh god, if I blog anonymously like Unpickled will someone figure out who I am? (Maybe.) Will my sister read it some day? (Probably). Do I need someone to talk to? (Yes.)

I set up a blog, name it after how I am feeling (tired of thinking about drinking), and I do something I've never done before. I reach out for sober help. *I try different.*

I begin here

It's July 8th, and this is the beginning of my 8th day sober. I've gone 9 days before, over a month ago. But never longer.

I'm starting this blog today because I suddenly realized last night that I was not going to make it . . . Me in my head alone is not going to get this done. I need to write it out. And I need to know that someone might read it. Doesn't matter who, someone. Someone out there might read this and might wonder if I stayed sober for another day.

~~~~~~

Source: Blog post, www.100daysoberchallenge.com/beginhere

Later that same day, I got my first blog comment from Cleo. Imagine that, there's *another* sober girl out in the sober universe. That might make three of us. I followed links and read her blog. I find that I can follow (stalk) other sober people. It is impossible to believe there are so many of us (and yet, really, the numbers were small then, there were maybe 15 sober bloggers, but this seemed gigantically huge because I'd thought it was only me. I'm the only one in the world who feels this way? Special. Unique. <sigh>).

I know that blogging isn't for everyone because it's all about writing honestly and openly, maybe for the first time in your life, about scary shitty stuff that you've told NO ONE, that you are sure NO ONE understands, and that you are certain that NO ONE has ever felt before. And you have to be able to write anonymously enough so that you don't fret.

For me, the accountability of blogging turned out to be hugely motivating. People come to a sober blog every day. They want to know how you are doing. I couldn't relapse with *ease* anymore. I couldn't say 'fuck it' weekly, nightly, like I had before. I had some vague form of accountability. And if I did relapse, I'd have to do it in front of an audience.

This kind of exposure can be brutal or it can be exciting. I'm in the exciting camp. You may not be. Don't read this section about me blogging and think "I can't/won't/don't want to blog, so this whole sober thing won't work for me."

[Are you still reading this, trying to find the ONE thing that you disagree with, so that you can say "this will never work for me." Yes, you. I can see you. I know you're there. So I'll tell you now: Keep reading.]

I did a lot of sober reading in my first weeks. And when I say a lot, I mean I was reading sober blogs from one to two hours a day. I discovered new people, followed links, read older posts from original Day 1s. I found people who'd relapsed and stopped posting, and I wondered how they were doing. Did they know we were still out here, haunted by their words, hoping they were well. Hoping they'd try again.

In a beautiful, tidy narrative, I'd now say something like this: I didn't want to go to AA, I knew there were others who didn't want to go to AA, there didn't seem to be many other options available to get sober support, so I *created the kind of change I wanted to see in the world. I wrote a sober blog that has now became a large, and super helpful sober community.*

All Maya Angelou and stuff. Of course that's only true in stories. And this isn't one of those kinds of stories.

THERE IS A GOOD STORY I can bring in though. I described my "Drink Now" voice on my blog, and someone reminded me of the two wolves:

An old Cherokee is teaching his grandson about life. "A fight is going on inside me," he said to the boy.

"It is a terrible fight and it is between two wolves. One is evil—he is anger, envy, sorrow, regret, greed, arrogance, self-pity, guilt, resentment, inferiority, lies, false pride, superiority, and ego." He continued, "The other is good—he is joy, peace, love, hope, serenity, humility, kindness, benevolence, empathy, generosity, truth, compassion, and faith. The same fight is going on inside you—and inside every other person, too."

The grandson thought about it for a minute and then asked his grandfather, "Which wolf will win?"

The old Cherokee simply replied, "The one you feed."

I named the drinking voice in my head 'Wolfie', though most days I don't dignify him with a capital letter. I began to say "fuck you Wolfie, I'm not drinking today." Think of the wolf in Little Red Riding Hood, dressed up like Gramma, trying to take you off the good path. Think of the wolf in the Three Little Pigs, trying to find cracks around windows, to blow your house down.

So I had two voices in my head. Wolfie and some version of a real me. Wolfie was loud and mean, and my voice was tiny.

Wolfie says: "You're a disaster, this is all too hard, you've had three weeks sober so you might as well drink now to celebrate."

The voice that is ME, says: "Maybe going to this party is not good idea."

Wolfie says to you: "You were held by the police overnight until you sobered up, but now it's a week later, and that will *never* happen again. I'll make sure that never happens again. You can have a few drinks and it'll be fine."

The voice that is YOU, when you're 50 days sober, says "I know sometimes I feel like drinking but I'm not going to because I don't want to have a new Day 1. I've done enough drinking in my past. I know that Day 1 is rotten."

The voice that is YOU says: "I want something different and better and I don't know what that is yet, but I know I want to try this sober thing."

Dehydrate the wolf

If you can picture booze like a Big Wolf With Black Eyes, he represents the voice in your head. Now you have to very calmly starve the wolf. Or better yet, you have to dehydrate him by not giving him anything to drink.

At first he'll be mad at you. "Where's my drink?"

You'll say: I have all this *free time* now. I can't talk to you, Wolfie. I'm running, baking, singing, reading, cleaning, spending time with my kids. I'm paying my taxes, cleaning off my desk, enjoying the weather.

The wolf will taunt you. "Everyone else is drinking, why can't you?"

You'll say: Sorry, Wolfie, can't hear you. I'm too busy cranking up the volume on my new iPad that I bought with *all the money I've saved*.

The wolf will throw temper tantrums. "Why can't I? What about now? When is this sober thing finished? Can I drink in a few more days? When exactly can I drink again?"

You'll say: I'm too busy snuggling with my husband, staying awake for conversations, I can see the look in his eyes, how proud he is of me, how supportive. I would never want him to look at me any other way, Wolfie, don't you understand that one glass of red wine does NOT equal my marriage? *I pick my marriage.* I pick it every day of the week and twice on Sundays. I pick meaningful conversations with friends. I pick sober laughing. It's the best. Have you tried it Wolfie? Sober laughing? You'll think you've died and gone to heaven.

The wolf will nearly be dehydrated. He'll try a few more last-chance, desperate attempts. "You're broken," he'll snarl. "You bitch, you can't be fixed, you'll always be a fuck-up, you suck at this, you might as well quit now."

And you'll say: You want to fight? I'll win. I've got so much *more energy now* that I'm sleeping through the night. I can outrun you Wolfie. I'm light on my feet now. I've got so much more spunk, clearer thinking. I'm planning to take over the world, Wolfie, me and my clear-headed genius.

What is that? Sorry I can't quite hear you. Your voice is so quiet, Wolfie. Are you nearly dehydrated? You're going to dry up and turn to dust. *Puts palm of hand up to lips and blows across the surface. Dust disperses, Wolfie is specks of grey in the air. And then gone.*

Source: Blog post, www.100daysoberchallenge.com/dehydrate

I completed Dry July and then felt nervous about drinking again, knowing how hard it had been to quit. I decided to extend my sober time. I went to three months. Then I added more. I had momentum, I kept going.

When I was around eight months sober, I offered to be penpals with other newly sober people. Turns out having more accountability is helpful—for you and for me. The number of penpals I had grew and grew (I remember wondering if there would ever be 100 people doing the 100-Day Sober Challenge).

By the time I was one year sober, I'd had 123 penpals.

I'm writing this now a few years later. Exchanging emails with penpals has turned me into a sort of sober coach (who knew!). Over the last few years, I've recorded hundreds of sober podcasts, a whack of daily one-minute sober messages, I've created a Sober Jumpstart class that comes with a responsive sober penpal, and—as of today— I have been penpals with 2,400+ people.

OK, LET'S WIND UP THIS HISTORY-ABOUT-ME PART. If you're dying to follow along with where I was on Day 21 or Day 58 or Day 242, or to see how the penpals and the coaching evolved in real time, you can get the first year of my blog in one big PDF file here: **www.100daysoberchallenge.com/pdf**. Did you see that shameless commercial link? I slipped it under the radar.

In the next sections, we'll talk about how my 100-Day Sober Challenge works, and get into the practical stuff of how, and why, and how, and "help me I feel crappy, and tell me what to do again."

PART 2. THINGS YOU NEED TO KNOW

IN THIS BOOK, I present the idea of doing a 100-Day Sober Challenge, which is something I've been hosting on my blog for years. If you're like me, you have a voice in your head that says "Drink Now," and you're wondering if that voice will stop if you quit drinking. (It will.)

I drank for a long time before I did a sober trial. I wanted to *want* to quit. Turns out that's not required.

To go forward now, you need only believe two things: that you drink more than you want to, and that you want to feel better.

You drink more than you want to. You have been unable to stick to rules that you create about how much you will consume. The quantity isn't even important. There's no measurement that says "a-ha there's a problem." There may be some small consequences to your over-drinking: disappointment in someone's eyes, missed opportunities, telling people at the dinner table about your husband's vasectomy, rushing through your daughter's bath time so that you can get back to your wine. Or you may have some larger repercussions: financial strain, marriage is in crisis, legal problems, escalating medical issues, or you've lost your driver's license.

You want to feel better. You're not sure if quitting drinking is the answer, and it might even seem like a drastic step, but you know this for sure: You want to feel better than you do now, and you're open to trying something new that will get you to a better-feeling place.

In Part 2 we'll be talking about the things you need to know to help with quitting drinking. Starting with "why be sober in the first place?"

SOBRIETY WANT AD

Benefits include great sleep, return of self-esteem, elimination of hangovers. Save $400 to $1,000 a month by not drinking. Double your money back if you hate being sober after hundreds of days.
For a limited time. Reach out now.
Operators are standing by.

Sobriety ~ It's not just for alcoholics anymore.

1. WHY BE SOBER?

Being sober is a relief.

Quitting drinking is like putting down a backpack of rocks that you've been carrying around for a long time. It's like a deep breath that fills your lungs.

Being sober is feeling proud of yourself.

Being sober is easier than drinking.

Too much of our brain space is used trying to manage alcohol consumption. The "Drink Now" voice is exhausting. All of that time we spend planning to drink—thinking about drinking, wondering how much alcohol there is, trying to figure out how we're going to get out of that work obligation because we're hungover—all of that can stop.

You have been drowning out who you really are. Literally. Banging yourself on the head with a bottle or two of wine. That's not you. The real you is in there. Drinking is a way of hiding from who you really are.

Here are some of the things to look forward to when you remove alcohol from your life: you feel better, you are proud of yourself, you sleep better, you spend less money, you consume fewer 'dumb' calories.

I have been a drinker before, and I've been a sober person. I can honestly say that being a non-drinker is unicorns and parades compared to drinking.

Carrie (day 21): "Being sober is like the smell of freshly baked bread every morning when I wake up. It's like the smell of fresh cut grass when I go outside. It feels like the last day of school . . . like stretching your legs after a long car journey when I get home . . . it's when someone puts a blanket on you just as you are about to fall asleep." [Update: She's on day 1,083 today.]

Resources:

Blog post ~ Being Sober is Like...,
www.100daysoberchallenge.com/beingsoberislike

Class ~ Sober Jumpstart: Lesson 1. Why Be Sober (22-minute audio),
www.soberjumpstart.com

2. PERMISSION TO QUIT

I click the link where it says: "Take this quiz to see if you're an alcoholic."

I scan and see the question about any legal problems related to alcohol. I have none. No missed work. Did I do any day drinking? Well, not unless you count brunch, vacations, or weekends. I calculate my online alcoholic score, and while I am perhaps drinking more than my allocated quantity any given week, I do not seem to meet the textbook definition of an alcoholic.

Relief.

Three days later I was online again. I knew something was up with me, and I continued my research by reading a few of the drunk women memoirs, and quickly found more confirmation:

Oh good, the woman in this book, this is not me either. There are so many things that happened to her that didn't happen to me. My drinking story lacks drinking from a paper bag under a bridge, sleeping on a park bench, and I haven't lost my job or my marriage.

And while no one feels they need permission to give up sugar—they decide what suits them, and then they do it—I was online looking for permission to quit drinking. I tried to find someone like me who'd quit and was happy about it, because I was worried that I would attract too much attention if I abruptly stopped ordering wine with dinner. Everyone would think that I had a PROBLEM. They wouldn't invite me to after-work-drinks because they'd think I was an ALCOHOLIC.

My life would have been easier, and I would have come to the idea of sobriety much more quickly and with less angst, if I had found a stop-drinking questionnaire that said something like: "It's OK to Quit Drinking. Nobody Needs to Drink."

In my fictitious world, the questionnaire would go like this:

1. Do you drink more than you want to? It's OK to stop.
2. Do you think about drinking all the time? I did too until I stopped.
3. Do you find it hard to quit? I did too. All the more reason to stop now.
4. Do you feel better when you don't drink? Not at first, maybe, but later—after seven to nine days sober, once all the booze and bullshit is gone, once you're hydrated again. Do you feel better then? Good. It's OK to stop.
5. Do you feel better sober than on a day with a hangover? Good. That's enough of a reason. You can stop.
6. Does your brain tell you to drink again to celebrate your sobriety? Mine too. It's OK, you can stay stopped.
7. Can you plan to drink again in some mysterious future time like 20 years from now if that's what it takes? Yes, you can NOT drink NOW.
8. Do you have to be an alcoholic to benefit from quitting drinking? No. Booze is an anaesthetic.

It changes who we are. It numbs and dulls and ultimately poisons.

9. Does anyone HAVE to drink? No.

10. Do you maybe need some advice and help and support to stop and stay stopped? Yes, I did.

Note: If you score 1 out of 10 or higher, it's OK to quit.

~~~~~~

Source: Blog post, www.100daysoberchallenge.com/questionnaire

---

from Unconfirmed Bachelorette (day 49): "Apparently, there are scores of people who want to give up, but don't because of the stigma. How asinine is that? 'I can't quit; they'll think I'm an alcoholic'. Or, 'there's no reason to quit unless you're an alcoholic' . . . I don't think I am, so I kept drinking. I've Googled the hell out of things like: Reasons to quit drinking even if you're not a real alcoholic; benefits of quitting drinking for non-alcoholics.

I was looking for permission to stop . . . maybe I am an alcoholic and I'm in denial. But my point is you do not have to fall into the 'real alcoholic' category, high bottom or low bottom or any bottom in between, to benefit from dropping the booze from your repertoire. You don't need to struggle with the 'real alcoholic'-or-not question. If you want to stop, stop. No labels required. I'm on day 49. I don't need an excuse to not drink." [Update: She's on day 420 today.]

Do we need to ask permission to stop pouring alcohol on our heads?

It doesn't matter what anyone else is doing. Just like the rest of your life, you can make the decision to not-drink. If you were a vegetarian—or running a marathon, or studying to be a nurse—you wouldn't need your husband or your best friend to do the same thing.

This is you the vegetarian:

You order lentils with a poached egg on top while your friend has eggs and bacon. If she says "don't you miss bacon" you smile sweetly and say: "sometimes I miss bacon, but I like how I feel when I don't eat meat." To be a vegetarian, you don't need your husband (or wife or your best friend) to join you. If you feel lonely or uninspired, then you take some time to read vegetarian cookbooks, listen to 'bacon is bad for you' podcasts, you find like-minded folks online, and you have a vegetarian coach who helps you find new inspiring recipes. [Please understand that this is only an example. I think that bacon is the world's perfect food.]

This is you the marathon runner:

You get up early to run, leave work on your lunch break to do a 10K loop. You head out in the rain, the dark, and the cold. You put on your headphones and you run. You figure out what to eat, when, what to wear, where to put the Vaseline. You don't need your husband (or wife or your best friend) to join you. You feel better when you run, so you do it. If you feel lonely or uninspired, you read running magazines, you listen to a podcast about a chick who lost 200 pounds and now runs marathons, you find like-minded folks online and you post your training schedule. You have a running coach whom you check in with daily to report your progress, get ideas, keep you motivated. [Please understand that this is an example, and while I have run one marathon in my life, it was a very long and dismal affair and I'm unlikely to do another one, ever. I do run regularly. But very sloth-like.]

This is you the nurse:

You are fascinated with home care, and elder care, and palliative care. You read books about it, you go to conferences. You study hard and you're compassionate and make great connections with your patients and their families. You don't need your husband (or wife or your best friend) to join you. If you feel lonely or uninspired or grief-stricken, you talk to your colleagues, you read some nursing magazines, you find a podcast of a nurse who works in oncology telling stories about their patients and how they cope.

And this is you sober:

You're not always sure what you're doing, where you're going, but you know that this is better for you. You don't want to feel like you did before. You've given up hangovers and replaced them with morning coffee. You've started collecting bulk teas. You can now drive your car after dinner (who does that?). You sleep through the night. You don't need your husband (or wife or your best friend) to join you. If you feel lonely or uninspired or freaked out or if Wolfie is yelling in your head, then you go online, you listen to an audio, you read some sober blogs, you email your sober penpal, you set up a call with your mentor.

Permission

If you are looking for explicit permission, I will state the obvious in case you've missed it:

You don't need anyone around you to join you. You do what's best for you. You don't need anyone's permission. You do what's best for you.

You have done plenty of alcohol research. You have tried making drinking rules. You've tried moderation. You've tried drinking. You know the results.

What you *haven't* tried is a longer period of sobriety research, to see if you like it, to see if you feel better (you will).

It's OK to not drink. Nobody *needs* to consume alcohol. Drinking is not required. You feel better without the booze. You can give it up.

~~~~~

Source: Blog post, www.100daysoberchallenge.com/permission

TRY THIS. Sometimes it's easier to hear a message in an audio. I've made up a one minute message for you and I really think you should stop and listen to it now. Nothing to download, just go to this link. You'll hear me talking directly to you.

Audio ~ One Minute Message 001: Stop Drinking,
www.100daysoberchallenge.com/stopaudio

3. THERE IS NO RIGHT TIME

Do you ever wake up and FEEL like doing the dishes? Hardly ever :) But if you run the water, pile up the plates, put on the music, and then get started you often find that doing the dishes isn't as bad as you thought.

So when do you start your 100-Day Sober Challenge? Today would be good. No waiting until the first of the month. No waiting until Monday. The time to start your sobriety research is now, because the sooner you begin, the sooner you will feel better. Your Wolfie brain will provide many reasons to delay: the upcoming party, vacation, work event, birthday. As far as Wolfie is concerned, there will always be an excuse to wait.

And that voice in your head? It's lying. It says: *You won't like being sober. You're not going to like feeling better. You're not going to like sleeping through the night. These sober people are ridiculous. They're happy, you're not. They're special, you're a fuck up.*

But the thing about Wolfie is that he's not very original. He says the same shit to everyone. We all hear the exact same voice. Those of us who are sober figure out how to get started, keep moving, and reach for support so that we're not sucked in by the voice.

The voice that says that this is bigger than you and that you're not smart enough, competent enough, ready enough, strong enough—it's all wrong.

You know how they say you quit drinking one day at a

time? That's because there is only (ever) today.

The only time you are making a decision to not drink is for this exact second, right now. You can't NOT drink tomorrow, or NOT drink yesterday. The only time you can NOT drink is right this minute. The only time you need to deal with the noise in your head, as it comes up, is right now. Am I going to drink now? No. Is that voice saying ridiculous things? Possibly. Am I going to learn to separate the Wolfie voice from the real me? Yes.

You probably don't know where to begin but you can learn it. You're worried that Wolfie won't ever shut up. He will. And yes, there will be a time when you don't think about drinking any more, not even when bad things happen.

---

from Dragonfly Wanders (day 0): "Can I seriously start again two days before Christmas?! I've been in a dark place. Away from home with in-laws I don't like. Gray and rainy, inside and out. Drinking to stay numb. Reaching out for a little support, Belle. Loved your podcast today. Felt like you were talking to me. Gonna get up and take a walk in the rain. Need to get out of my head."

me: You can definitely start right now. The sooner you start, the sooner you feel better. Today can be Day 1. You can leave the darkness behind you. Rain is good. Reaching out is good too.

from AnnieUK: "My latest thought has been: Well, I'm never going to succeed when my vacation is only a couple of weeks away, so why start now? But then I'll go on this trip, drink a lot, feel bad, upset my kids, my parents . . . and need to address it all again in a few weeks time, no further forward. So, I should start now? Build some strength. But do I have ANY strength?"

me: There is no tomorrow. Tomorrow is today. The sooner you start, the sooner you feel better. You don't have to have the strength yourself, that's what having support is for. A meeting (I know you don't want one), a visit with your doctor, a counsellor, a call with me, do my Sober Jumpstart class. You need to add some supports in, before you get too sad. huglets from me

4. NEVER AND FOREVER

from M: "I worry about the idea of *never* being able to have another drink again. I know I am better not drinking, I don't know how I will be able to NEVER have another drink again. Even the thought of it . . ."

When I first quit drinking, other sober bloggers would tell me that I'd eventually stop thinking about alcohol. I thought they were exaggerating (or flat out lying). *What if at some future time there's a death, are you telling me that I won't want to drink then?* A long-term sober girl said "yes, that's what happened to me. My father died and I didn't even think of drinking." She didn't even THINK of it? Really?

When I first quit, I made a deal with myself to get to my goal, and then I would reassess if I wanted to continue or not. First up, I wanted to do Dry July. Then when I arrived at 30 days, I thought, "I still feel weird, I can't tell if I should go back to drinking or if I should keep doing this sober thing, so I will extend the sober trial to 90 days."

I hit 60 days sober, and something pretty weird happened. My daily mental obsession about NOT drinking had eased considerably. When I became sober penpals with thousands of people, I then had my suspicions confirmed by hundreds of other people. They too were experiencing the same thing: Something shifts after Day 60, and the mental obsession eases dramatically.

Wolfie pokes his head in periodically, sure, but by Day 60 I was able to say, "I'm not drinking for now. I have too much to do. Too many things to accomplish. Ask again later, Wolfie. The answer for now is NO."

When I got to 90 days, I said: "I will go a bit longer." At around eight and a half months, I went through a serious temper tantrum period where the whole idea of being sober seemed ridiculous, and I had many days of feeling that the whole experiment had been pointless and a waste of time. A few days later, I felt better.

Then my new plan was to drink when I got to my one year soberversary. You can predict maybe what happened when I got to a year. I said: "Am I going to give up this wonderful sober thing now and go back to Day 1? Yuck. Maybe I'll wait a bit longer."

By then, Wolfie was pretty darn quiet. Sober people had told me it would happen; we end up in a place where even if bad shit happens, we do NOT think about drinking. I had arrived there.

Wolfie was quiet and I had NO desire to wake him up.

Even now I still don't say that I've quit drinking forever. I've just moved the finish line. Any time I have a weird twinge and Wolfie says "maybe one glass," I say to myself: "You're not quitting forever. You're quitting for now. You can drink again in 21 years when you retire if you still feel like it later. Not today. Got too much to do."

I understand that this sounds completely ridiculous, but my brain accepts it as reasonable. I say to myself "it's not that I can't drink, it's that I'm not drinking now because I have stuff to do."

You have things to do, too. Kids to take care of, jobs to excel at, companies to build. You want to move across the country, pay more attention to your marriage, finish the degree, train the dog, carve the headboard, write the song.

You have reasons why you need to be sober right now. To feel better, to repair things, to feel proud of yourself. And in order to circumvent the complex and sticky question of 'is this forever', you tell yourself that you'll drink *later*, in some imaginary future time. But you're not drinking now. Not today.

---

from K: "What I like about the Sober Challenge is that it is 100 days—not forever. In the past, I have gone from drinking my brains out, to saying I am going to stop forever. And then an enticing opportunity to drink would arise and I would think, '*forever can start tomorrow*, or after XYZ event.' A hundred days is a very short time compared to forever, and for now it is a number that seems more significant than 30 and easier to swallow than, say, 365."

5. SENSITIVE

As a group, we tend to be super sensitive—to emotions, to feeling overwhelmed, to fatigue. My sensitivity looks like this: I'm ticklish, get motion sick easily, feel like I'm going to kill someone if I get too hungry (not just *hangry*, but murderous). I am easily startled, not a fan of mice or bats, I am prone to anxiety, I have a hard time with repetitively irritating noises like taps dripping, and I am a very light sleeper who needs the right pillow.

Do you see how I'm telling you about me? I'm doing that on purpose. It's easier to read about how wacky *I* am. It's less jarring than if I come right out and say: *You are more sensitive than most people.*

If I write it like that, you think you're broken, or there's something wrong with you. When I tell you about me, it seems entertaining because it's THAT OTHER PERSON.

I'm emotionally sensitive, oh god, about everything. My feelings are easily hurt, I cry when happy or sad. I'm easily offended, irritated, sensitive to criticism, impatient. But also emotionally intuitive, I can tell at a dinner party who's feeling ignored. I can see that she loves her husband.

I am an over-thinker. I get stuck in logic loops. I want to analyze problems (for hours, years) before I try to implement any strategies to see if they'll work. I like to read about doing things more than I like doing them. I have a brain that believes that rehearsing future events somehow helps me.

I have an anxious stomach. Before a flight, before a presentation. In a car. I feel tense when I know that my alarm is going to go off at 5 a.m. so that I can get up to write this sober book. I'm a compulsive watch checker.

You.

You are probably a sensitive human, too. You probably feel pain more deeply, hold on to resentments longer. You've been accused by shitty friends of being a cry baby. You are probably a crappy sleeper, or have nervous guts, or you wear only black because it's less visually disturbing. Let's say that I feel better without a lot of chaos. I'm a clean surface girl. I like one piece of tape on the envelope instead of three.

You. We.

We are more sensitive than other people. And so, yes, we have sought out ways to soothe that over-sensitivity. We used the tools we had available—perhaps not great tools— but we didn't know any better. Alcohol works in that it dulls our easily startled, over-sensitive brains. But it dulls everything else, too. Booze is a blunt instrument. It's like a hammer. Banging on our head. Anaesthetizing.

Our sensitivities make us a difficult bunch. For example, if you offer to help me but you don't ask me the 'right' way, I'll say no automatically. We bristle at playing the 'reindeer' games at the office but then resent when we're not included in said games.

It's hard to be prickly and sensitive AND also want to be sober, because our natural gut-instinct, first-response, default answer is: "That won't work for me."

It may be frustrating to you when I say that we're very similar, as a group, those of us who drink too much. Because you don't *want* to be the same as everyone else. Your situation is different, you say. Your particular problems are worse. Your challenges are specifically heinous.

In fact, we have substantially more in common than any of the small details that may distract us into thinking that we're different. Married or not married. Kids or no kids. Male or female or gay or old or young.

You are part of this 'sensitive' group, and *this is good news*, because it means that some of what has worked for me and my sober penpals might also work for you.

It also means that you are not alone. Someone out there DOES understand what it's like to be you. And I'll talk more about self-soothing, treats, and how we can feel better in upcoming sections.

~~~~~~~~~

Resource:
Audio ~ One Minute Message 035: Orchid,
www.100daysoberchallenge.com/orchid

---

from Sparkly23: "Listening to your audios is a HUGE help. You talk about the common thread & typical experiences most everyone goes through. *Here I was thinking I was so alone in this crappy drinking prison.* The more research I do, I'm stunned with the similarities in everyone's story."

6. YOU WILL FEEL SHITTY FOR THE FIRST WEEK

When you stop drinking, you may feel like you have the flu for the first week or so. Headache, fatigue, dehydration, poor concentration, some foggy thinking. It does get better (and quickly) but the first seven to nine days can be weird.

To make it easier on yourself, you can—right now—give up the idea of getting stuff done, like housekeeping, like making dinner. Take a deep breath and sigh with relief when you realize that for the first week sober, you will only do laundry if absolutely necessary. You hereby have permission to vegetate on the couch and watch Netflix. And yes, you can skip making dinner for a week. Pasta with jarred sauce. Frozen macaroni. Take-out.

In this first week of (probably) feeling unwell, try to sleep as much as you can. Your poor body needs time to rest, repair, reset, recover. I often slept 12 hours at a time in my first month sober. I also went to bed at 7:30 p.m., fully clothed, to escape from life when it seemed like I'd run out of things to do.

This will sound obvious but I'll say it anyway. Try to do a lot less of everything, especially in the first few weeks. Ask for help. Find someone to drive the kids to swimming lessons. Order your groceries online if being in the store is awkward. Do as little at work as you can without being fired. Practise saying 'no'—no I can't water your plants while you're away this week, sorry. No, I can't do three extra loads of laundry because you cleaned out your dresser today. No, I can't volunteer for that new work thing, not right now, not this week.

You are going to email me and say "is it normal to feel so tired?" I'll say yes. "Is it normal to feel like I'm sick?" I'll say yes.

---

from Taylor (day 11): "You hear 'you'll be an emotional roller coaster' and to me I thought it would be something like PMS. But I've had moments of rage, and then I've had moments where I want to cry, or moments of rage and crying at the same time. I'm also very happy. And I want to change. But I'm very sad so that's throwing me off."

me: You're sad because you're losing your friend, alcohol?

T: "Definitely."

me: Or you're sad because your life is rotten with alcohol and now you'd like to feel better?

T: "Yes."

You're breaking up with alcohol. Good riddance. Let yourself have some time to feel crappy. You may well feel like you've lost a 'friend'. Alcohol isn't your friend, though. It's more like a toxic ex-boyfriend who says "It'll be different this time, I promise."

And even when bad relationships end, you may feel adrift. This is normal. It takes a while for your life to flow back into the space that booze occupied. You've had an alcohol-ectomy. You've been drinking for a while. Give yourself some time to feel better. Be patient.

Because this is a common question, and a frequent worry, you'll notice that I talk about this again in Parts 3 and 4 later in this book.

~~~~~~~~~~~

Resources:

Audio ~ One Minute Message 016: Patience, www.100daysoberchallenge.com/patience

Blog post ~ Toxic, www.100daysoberchallenge.com/toxic

7. PLAN A REPLACEMENT DRINK

There is a point in each day when you will most feel like drinking. I call this the *witching hours*. Typically it's around dinner time; for me it was 6:00 p.m. to 8:30 p.m.

If you were to plot the duration of the witching hours on a graph, the period of time gets predictably shorter and less intense each day. Like, Day 1 might be 2 hours of hand-wringing, and then the next day it's 1.75 hours, and then 1.5 hours.

Having a replacement drink is a good idea. Your brain is used to having something to drink at this time of day, so you can plan a lovely replacement drink. I have found that bitter drinks deal with cravings better than sweet drinks. I'm sure there's a scientific reason why, but for me "bitter is better." Think grapefruit juice and tonic water, cranberry and lime. Don't give me *any* nonsense about the price of bottled drinks. I know what whiskey costs and I know what red wine costs. Imported bottled water is less expensive. A litre of no-name tonic water is cheap. Little cans of fancy lemonade are a bargain. You can make homemade Fuck You Wolfie lemonade with rosemary [**www.100daysoberchallenge.com/lemonade**].

What about non-alcoholic beer?

I avoid fake beer, fake wine, and other non-alcoholic drinks or de-alcoholized beverages. There is often a small percentage of alcohol in supposedly non-alcoholic drinks (often as much as 0.5%).

But most importantly, I don't drink NA beverages because I do not want my brain to even *think* it's having alcohol. I don't want to fake-drink. I don't even pour sparkling water into a wine glass, I use a regular juice glass.

I think mock-drinking in any form is a slippery-slopey bad idea. No fizzy fake champagne. No little bottles of apple juice that look like beer.

Let it be said that there are many people in the sober world who do consume NA drinks and they say that it is fine *for them*. And it may well be fine (for them). Me personally, I continue to err on the side of caution. I have spent time trying to get Wolfie to shut up, so I am not going to risk waking him up for the sake of a fake drink made to look like alcohol.

There are some situations or events where you are used to having wine, and if you replace the wine with something else, the absence is felt less (yes, I know, it's not the same to have ginger ale when your brain wants wine, but it's a partial replacement: it's a beverage in a glass). You used to watch (and sleep through) a movie with wine in your hand. Now you can watch (and remember) a movie with tonic and lime. It's not the wine that makes the movie better. You want the snuggle-cosy-alone-time that a movie brings. Turns out it doesn't matter what's in your glass. You drink lemonade, or imported mineral water, or tea.

8. TREATS AND REWARDS

When I first quit drinking, things felt upside down. My favourite coping strategy for life had been removed. I felt like a clam without a shell.

While everyone said 'it gets easier' I didn't have the capacity to believe them. I felt like a strong wind was going to knock me over, tip me backwards, and pour booze down my throat.

The only way I could convince myself that being sober was worth it, was to have a treat or a reward. Not a buy-a-car reward. Not a get-a-book-if-still-sober-in-three-months reward.

We are so used to using alcohol as our only treat, that we need to learn new treats. And if you don't reward your sobriety with something else, then Wolfie will come in with "you can celebrate sobriety with a drink, since you've done so well."

When I first quit, I needed an every-second-day treat. I got myself fresh fruit, perhaps for the sugar cravings, perhaps because I am lazy and there is a *fruterie* at the end of my street. I bought myself half a pineapple. Then two days later, a tiny overpriced ridiculously delicious container of raspberries. Then I saw the golden raisin nut mix at the organic store and bought a scoop of that wrapped up in a brown paper package.

Your sober treats do not need to be food. You can have bubble bath, trashy magazines, flowers, oven mitts, bad

TV from Netflix, time alone, cheap earrings, or savoury pancakes. Perhaps you'll plan to have steak every Friday for the first six weeks. And if you don't eat steak, then substitute salmon or sushi or marinated tofu in that category. Don't get hung up on the word 'steak'. The goal is to have something to look forward to.

from Soberman (day 3): "The idea of getting treats was a tough one. When I read it at first, I was like: 'Why do this? I buy what I want when I want to (not true), and I am indeed not a foodie, blah blah. Are you trying to lure me into some girly spin on simple, plain awareness and self-care? No manly adventures or big storytelling?' Ha. But I started drafting my list of treats and I soon had this warm feeling about every task and 'sensing' situation that I love—and have forgotten. The all too expensive original luxury British Ginger Beer, ice cold, tall glass with extra ice. That extra polish and wax luxury carwash, as the car deserves it and I enjoy it afterwards. A huge cappuccino coffee for myself at some café while planning the upcoming week (and the next set of treats!)"

You might mistakenly believe that your brain doesn't respond to treats and rewards. There is often resistance to my treat idea. You will say: "I have to save money. I live out in the country so it's hard for me to shop. I already buy myself whatever I want. I have to lose weight. I don't deserve a reward for being sober." Let's address some of this Wolfie-thinking:

I have to save money. You spent money drinking, so you can invest some of those Wolfie dollars to support your sobriety. You can get some consumables like tea, take-out coffee, perfume, or sober socks. You have a few dollars to spend every second day on your sobriety, to reinforce your sober choices, to support you as you do this hard thing. If Wolfie tells you that you can't afford to buy yourself nice cherry jam, then he's a bastard liar. And you can tell him I said so. Ha.

And the every-two-day treats thing, it's not forever. It's until you get going, perhaps for the first 16 days and again during times of stress, or when you're feeling wobbly.

I still use treats from time to time, whenever I'm having a rough patch or to get through something hard. I'm three and a half years sober, and I'm using treats RIGHT NOW to help me write this book. I find writing—like early sobriety—to be confusing sometimes. Thankfully my brain isn't very smart, and I respond to sober writing treats like take-out lunch on Wednesdays and flowers on Fridays and a movie on Sunday. These are my treats for writing this book. I think we could agree that it's working.

Sober treats won't work for me because I already buy myself everything I want. That's fine. You can continue to buy the same things, just frame them differently. As you pick up the expensive ground coffee in the grocery store, you can say to yourself "this is my treat for being sober." Later when you drink the coffee, you repeat the same message to yourself.

You think that your brain isn't going to respond to coffee or jam or lipstick? It will. It does. It responds to mint tea, too. The first few times you have mint tea, you're thinking "this doesn't work," but you keep repeating to yourself: "this is my treat for being sober." And then a few days later, after dinner, your brain pipes up with "where's my mint tea?"

---

from S: "Here are some examples of things I've treated myself to: fuzzy blankets, silver jewelry, deluxe candles, essential oils, chocolate croissants, lovely beads, thrift shopping, craft supplies, gourmet ground coffee, a gorgeous teacup, a bouquet of flowers, a potted basil plant. The largest was a countertop dishwasher. The trick is to either find something that you want but don't need, or to splurge on a more deluxe version of something you were going to buy anyway. Like shampoo or lipstick. I have always struggled with confidence and my inner critic is a real bitch. The concept of self-care is relatively new to me and these gifts remind me to treat myself kindly."

I have to lose weight so I can't buy chocolate. You're going to throw this book across the room now. Ready? There is no weight loss in early sobriety. It does happen, yes, but it happens later. Being sober is the key to other things. It is the lead domino. Being sober makes other things *possible*. To focus on weight loss right away is not only crazy-making, it's unrealistic, distracting, beside-the-point, and it makes Wolfie leap in with his booming voice yelling: "this is all too hard."

There's a non-statistical, barely anecdotally-based *certainty* in my inbox, that says if I get an email from a sober penpal saying "I can't have treats because I'm trying to lose weight" then I will get a corresponding email several days (or weeks) later that says "can you reset me on Day 1 today, Wolfie got to me, this is hard."

[Beware. When you hear "This is all too hard" it signals that you are feeling overwhelmed. Too many things at once, might as well drink. More in Section 10: Avoid 'Overwhelm'.]

People who figure out the sober treats idea do better. They're more successful at being sober. They have an easier time. So you want to figure this out.

~~~~~~~~~

Resources:

Blog post ~ Gold Stickers, www.100daysoberchallenge.com/gold

Blog post ~ Treat-erator, www.100daysoberchallenge.com/treats

Video ~ Treats, www.100daysoberchallenge.com/treatsvideo

Class ~ Sober Jumpstart: Lesson 4. Treats & Rewards (20-minute audio), www.soberjumpstart.com

9. WHO TO TELL AND WHAT TO SAY

> **from Potato Girl (day 158):** "One of my friends has been texting that she wants to visit, and says: 'we can drink A LOT of wine! I need a break!' I know she will be supportive of me, but I am avoiding telling her that I am sober."

In the beginning, I didn't want anyone to know that I wasn't drinking. I felt nervous. *They'll think I'm un-fun. They'll think I have a problem.* I was terrified of any scrutiny as to why I was sober. I was nervous that someone was going to pressure me to drink.

When I first quit, I said "I've quit drinking until I lose 20 pounds." Then when friends saw me next, and I hadn't lost any weight, they were silent on the subject. Who wants to comment on someone's apparently lack of success in dieting?

Later, I graduated to saying, "I'm doing a self-discipline challenge, which means no alcohol for three months." Mostly when I said that, people would change the subject to talk about THEMSELVES, and about how they wished they could quit smoking, or run a marathon, or do something that they perceived to be along the same vein.

Even now, when I meet someone for the first time, and I say that I don't drink, if asked, I explain it like this: "I found that alcohol—even one drink—affected my sleep. I was waking up a lot in the middle of the night. When I started catering, I hated my life when I got up to bake bread at 6 a.m. and I hadn't had enough sleep. So I gave up the wine. I know, it's hard to believe but it's true. I actually picked catering over wine." And then I smile.

If cornered by a weird brother in-law or a boozing friend who won't stop needling you, then I think it's totally fine to invent something. Antibiotics are always good. Just say 'yeast infection' and that tends to shut people up.

I think you should say what you want, when you want, and how you want. If you DO want to say something more, and you want to tell people that you're in recovery, or that you're an alcoholic, or that you go to AA, or that you've been to rehab—then please say it.

As well, I fully support you NOT telling people if you don't want to. I didn't even tell my husband what I was doing for weeks because I felt too fragile and embarrassed and unsure. I had many doubts about my ability to remain sober, and didn't want to admit that to my husband. He's a good guy, supportive. The problem was in my head. I was too weird and scared on the inside. I wasn't ready for scrutiny or questions, at least not in the beginning. I think we finally talked about it when I was on Day 17 [see link to the blog post in the Resources for this section].

WHILE EVERYONE WORRIES about what they'll say when asked, I was honestly disappointed when I realized that most people didn't give a shit if we drink or not. If someone is a 'normie' (a normal drinker), they often don't drink, they go weeks at a time without alcohol. The fact that you're not drinking tonight is boring to them.

Some of your friends who are boozers may feel a little threatened, as they perhaps wonder what this means for them. "Can I still drink? Will it bother you if I drink in front of you?" Their Wolfie will want to pave the way to ensure that no matter what the fuck *you're* doing, it won't have any impact on their ability to have the next glass and the next.

Between those two groups—normies and boozers— most other people mind their own business. You may get the occasional question. When I meet people for the first time and say "I don't drink," no one says anything. I've had two pointed questions in my three years sober. From my brother-in-law: "So, can I ask, why aren't you drink- ing?" I gave him my story about sleeping, saying it was easier to have none.

The second question came from the wife of a friend. She's the one from the "A glass wall of alcohol" blog post I have reprinted at the end of this section. During a recent visit, she said "so you're still not drinking, how is it? We're drinking a lot less now than we used to. Do you miss it?"

In this case, I shared more than I normally would. You will know when someone is truly asking you what it's like to be sober, so that they can picture doing it themselves. This is different from someone who is being curious or prying into your personal business.

To this friend, I said that the first few weeks were tough (she nods) and that to begin there always seemed to be an occasion where drinking would seem like a good idea (yes, yes), but that once we opened a bottle it was too easy to finish it and open the second one. "That's where we are now," she says. We are understanding each other. I know what she's asking (*is it possible, will I like it, can it be done*) and she knows what I'm saying (*we were drinking too much, now we've stopped entirely, it's much better*). I don't have to reach out and take her hand. I don't have to say anything. Just me being sober, she can see that it's possible. When I quit, I didn't know one sober person who quit before a low bottom. This woman, she knows me.

So in instances like this, I share more. Normal drinkers don't care. Boozers are sometimes shitty but it's their Wolfie talking. You will come up with a version of the story that you can tell that works for you.

A glass wall of alcohol

In this city where we are visiting, in this city where we used to live, we had dinner last night with a long-time drinking friend. The guy (and his wife) drink a lot. A shit lot. Even when we were drinking, too, we never drank as much as these two. The four of us would hang out, yes, but I'd always watch the guy and marvel/feel sick at the quantities he'd put away. The ordering 'another round' even after we'd already said we were done. Telling me he loved me at a particularly sloppy party. The disclosing of sexual details during a meal.

Last night, they had beer before the meal, a bottle of wine during, and opened a second bottle after. [This is exactly what we would have done, too.]

Mr. Belle was nervous to arrive with our three cans of tonic water. The couple joked with us, saying that by the end of the night they would have 'pushed us off the wagon'. But really, once they got drinking, they weren't the least bit interested in what we were doing, whether we were drinking or not.

By 10:30 p.m. I was tired and ready to go home, and I tapped Mr. B's foot under the table. The guy looks to his wife and says (re the second bottle of wine), "have some more, it's open."

I looked at their glasses of wine. I looked at them talking loudly over each other, each vying for our attention, "let me tell the story, no let me. Did you see the episode where . . .?"

In the car on the way home, I told Mr. B that I was sorry that they talked 'at' him, instead of 'to' him. They didn't ask questions about his work or his life in Europe or about how things are going for us. Instead it seemed like they struggled and competed to tell him about every single thing that had happened to them since we saw them last, including punchlines to badly remembered jokes; including repeating things seen on YouTube.

Honestly, the evening was like a comedy show except it wasn't funny. Yeah, it was like the *worst* kind of stand-up comedy. People trying to make a connection, and failing gigantically, because they are behind a *glass wall of alcohol*. They kept talking even if Mr. B needed clarification. They ignored Mr. B when he spoke, and literally jostled each other if one tried to interrupt the other. And on. And on.

Nothing of any real substance or connection or interest was shared. No real questions were asked or answered. No one felt touched, or brought together, or connected.

Looking into that glass wall of alcohol, I saw a mirror. And it was grim.

Did it make me want to drink?

No.

We used to be that couple, too. That used to be us.

~~~~~

Source: Blog post, www.100daysoberchallenge.com/glasswall

Resources:

Class ~ Sober Jumpstart: Lesson 3. Who to Tell and What to Say (18-minute audio), www.soberjumpstart.com

Blog post ~ The conversation with my husband on day 17, www.100daysoberchallenge.com/husband

Blog post ~ Thanks for giving me a yeast infection, www.100daysoberchallenge.com/yeast

10. AVOID 'OVERWHELM'

One of the reasons we drink is in search of an 'off' switch: to quiet our brains, to escape responsibilities, to have 'me' time.

If there are coping strategies that are adaptive (make things better) versus maladaptive (make things worse), then drinking is maladaptive. While it may be an off-switch, it creates many other problems at the same time.

It'd be like saying: I'm bored (problem) and so I'm going to slam my hand in a car door so that I'm not bored any more (maladaptive, makes things worse).

A better approach would be: I'm bored (problem), and so I'm going to clean out one drawer in the kitchen (adaptive, helps with boredom, doesn't create a new problem, makes things better).

I have many theories, mostly unsupported and more like hunches based on my own experience and those of my penpals. While I know that the plural of anecdote is not data, I *have* seen some patterns and I think they mean something. Someone with a PhD in Importance should come in and study this.

As younger humans, maybe age 9 to 12, in the face of something chaotic or traumatic, or at a time where we felt like we didn't fit in, or where we sensed that it wasn't OK to *just be us*, right at that time, we felt crappy and wanted to have some way of feeling better. We're not very well developed at this age and we reach for things that make us feel better, that distract us, and some of the tools we use are adaptive, and some aren't.

We crush on teen idols like Donny Osmond (that was me!), numb out by reading teen runaway novels (me), and we take up some kind of bad habit that has the effect of distancing us from reality (for me it was smoking, at age 12; yes, I know).

For lots of people, this is a time when eating disorders, or cutting, or drugs, or alcohol come in. We are not taught, explicitly, how to deal with uncomfortable feelings, or how to self-soothe. So we reach for available tools, however malformed.

Did your parents ever sit you down and have a conversation with you about what you can do if you feel overwhelmed, exhausted, irritated, freaked out, lonely, or depressed? Did they give you strategies and tools to help you with Changing the Channel in Your Head? No. Mine neither. Did they model for you how they dealt with disappointment, their feelings of not fitting in, or how they coped with the occasional overwhelming sense of dread? If they did model for you, was it with something other than cigarettes, alcohol, drugs, or a bucket of Kentucky Fried Chicken? Did your parents have 'self-care' time where they made it clear that they needed to recharge batteries, to unwind. Did they lock themselves in the tub with big mounds of lavender bubble bath and candles? Did your father go for a run when he was feeling stressed, or to delineate the mark between 'work' and 'home' and did he *tell* you he was doing this, explicitly, so that you could learn to do the same? No? (Where are my fictitious PhD researchers when I need them. Can you come in and study what happens when you teach adaptive self-care strategies to preteens, particularly those in chaotic, addictive, impoverished, or violent homes? Thanks. I'll wait for your results.)

So in your first months sober, you will get a crash course in adaptive self-care strategies, whether you want it or not.

One of the most important things you will do is learn to strategically avoid 'overwhelm'—I use this word as a noun, it's a thing on the horizon, like fog.

Your life is like a video game. You can see potential bombs, things advancing, that could blow up and throw you off course. Your job is to navigate them. You don't walk right into a bomb and hope for the best. You don't test yourself by repeatedly doing difficult or stressful things. Instead, you ask someone to carpool, you decline social activities, and you simplify meals.

Your job is to *reduce overwhelm*. All around you, there are lists of things to do and when you first quit drinking you are going to take it easy. You will shower once a day, try not to get fired, and skip everything else.

Thinking that you need to push or force yourself to do things is a holdover from your drinking time, when you were hungover and you made yourself do things to prove that you didn't have a problem. You wanted to make yourself look normal. You took on more than you could reasonably do, so that you looked high-functioning, so that nobody knew how much you were drinking, and so no one could detect how you felt about yourself.

When you first quit drinking, you are going to remember that being overwhelmed is our number one trigger. You will instead do less. Learn to be slothful. Embrace the art of underachieving.

> **from Marsha H (day 14):** "Belle, I am sober. Today I am reducing overwhelm by skipping two small events that were stressing me out. I found that it was the old me obeying the 'voice of I HAVE TO GO THERE AND DO THIS'."

Here are my top three tools for overwhelm: exercise, tub, and bed. I probably use exercise four times a week, specifically to help with my mood. I'm in the tub anytime I'm feeling antsy, or as my reward at the end of a day of catering. And as far as sleep is concerned, I have been known to go to bed at 7:30 p.m. in early sobriety, because I had no other way of dealing with life. I knew I didn't want to drink, and I had no idea what else to do except 'hide'.

I still use sleep for hiding. This week (was it three days ago?), this book writing thing wasn't going well, I was having a shit day, and I was in bed at 5:30 p.m., fully clothed, waiting to feel better. I napped for about half an hour, and got up and kept going.

Oh I can't nap, I have two children, I have a big job, I have . . .

Ask your sister to watch your kids while you have an hour alone at the mall. (If she's not available, you can lock yourself alone in the bathroom for a while.) If you're at work, you get up and go for a 'coffee' as a way of decompressing, walk around the block a few times. You remove yourself from the situation until you can see clearly again. At a party, you get up and play with the dogs, or go outside.

When you first quit drinking, you will feel wacky, raw and exposed. So you will want to strive for underwhelm. It will take some practise, and your ability to see things in advance will improve as you're sober. For now, aim for sloth. Do a lot less.

~~~~~~~~~~

Resources:

Audio ~ Sober Podcast 001: Accepting Help,
www.100daysoberchallenge.com/SP001

Audio ~ Sober Podcast 005: A Shitstorm of Treats,
www.100daysoberchallenge.com/SP005

Audio ~ Sober Podcast 038: Overwhelm,
www.100daysoberchallenge.com/SP038

Audio ~ Sober Podcast 040: Cinnamon Toast,
www.100daysoberchallenge.com/SP040

Audio ~ Sober Podcast 080: Blowing a Fuse,
www.100daysoberchallenge.com/SP080

11. CHANGE THE CHANNEL IN YOUR HEAD

from Imara (day 14): "Happy to have made it through my first 2 weeks. They were REALLY LONG. Time drags all evening and going to bed early isn't easy. But feeling good about myself and so happy to keep on going . . . Did some yoga and may hit the gym to get out and distract myself for a while. Cooking and cleaning isn't doing it. Tomorrow's another day, and so I go soberly into the future :)"

me: There isn't one big fix. There are a bunch of small fixes that we rotate through depending on our mood each day. Some days cooking and cleaning will help. Other days it'll be yoga. Then it'll be a bath. And then listening to music.

I first learned the idea of 'changing the channel' from Tony Robbins, the tall guy with the big hands. In one of his books, he talks about changing states and how we try to adjust our mood when we start to feel low (or weird or shitty or overwhelmed). The first 100 days of being sober has a range of emotions, fluctuations in enthusiasm, and moods that can go up and down.

Robbins said that we heavily rely on three ways to change our state: drugs, alcohol, and shopping. I would put sex in there too, and other potentially addictive activities, like gambling.

If you feel anxious or overwhelmed or exhausted or sad or afraid, what do *you* do to change the channel? Yes, you personally.

You used to drink (past tense, you're learning new things now).

So did I. For me, it was cigarettes and alcohol. Driving in the car, bored, smoke. Lull at work, bored, smoke. Home after work, exhausted, drink, and smoke. Watch bad TV, smoke, drink. Weekends spent shopping for food I didn't cook. Knitting projects abandoned. On repeat.

And you might say, "but Belle, I don't have any other way to deal with being in a terrible mood, or depressed, or overtired, and I have to unwind right now. "

When we are drinking, we use alcohol to fix every-thing—or so we think—and we don't develop any other self-soothing, comforting, or change-the-channel tools.

Turns out—who knew—there are at least 578 other ways to shift how you feel. There are things you've done before, perhaps by accident, things that once you remember them, and try them, you think "OK, good, I feel better." Like when you change the sheets on the bed you feel better. And when you have a nap you feel better. And when you snuggle on the couch with a fluffy blanket and braid your cats' tails together you feel better. Especially if you add hot chocolate.

So right now you can stop and make a list of three things (of the possible 578 choices) that you could do to change the channel in your head when you are bored, tired, excited, anxious, or agitated. Things you can do instead of drinking:

1. _____

2. _____

3. _____

How about dance? Did you put that on your list? Play loud music (that's one) and then dance around the living room (that's two), singing very loudly (that's three). You can play piano (four).

It's not only the fact that playing piano *distracts* you. The act of playing itself makes you feel better. You like playing piano. *You feel better when you do it.*

You have many of these 'feel better when you do it' things. You have forgotten what they are. Booze flows in, regular life and regular coping strategies flow out. Remove the booze, stand there for a few moments thinking, "what now?"

What now. You do other things. You have your replacement drink. You dig in the garden, scrub the garage floor, clean the bathtub. Decluttering is surprisingly therapeutic (cleaning from the outside-in).

How long is your list of activities to change the channel now that you're thinking about it consciously? You thought the only way to unwind was with a drink. That is what Wolfie tells us, and it turns out that Wolfie is a lying bastard.

I know this whole section seems ridiculous, but when we're feeling ginormously bad, we can't think of anything to do that would make us feel better. So right here, right now, you are going to make a list (while you're feeling relatively OK) so you can look at it later (when you're feeling shitty and think that drinking is the *only* solution to *all* of life's problems).

A change of location works. If you're at home, go out. If you're out, go home :) If you're alone, get with some people. If you're overwhelmed in a group, hide in the bathroom and read sober blogs on your phone. Yes, really.

Reading is good. *There's no frigate like a book.* You read five or ten pages and that might be long enough to change the channel, turn the knob on the radio dial a few millimetres to the left, and now you hear a new station, a better station, one with calming soothing loving you're-going-to-be-fine messages.

When I first read Tony Robbins' book, I made a list of the ways to change my state. It had 30+ things on it. They included: listen to loud music, play guitar, sing, talk on the phone, write a letter longhand, take a bath with candles, light candles anywhere in the house, clean my desk, clean anything, go for a run, make tea, plan meals, test a recipe, read a magazine, brainstorm with clients, design a new logo, read light fiction, read self-help, make a puzzle, go for a walk, take pictures, go swimming, watch a good movie, go to a concert, go to see a movie at the theatre with popcorn, listen to podcasts, do volunteer work, find an audience and do some kind of public speaking, write in my journal, play cards, explore a new part of the city, go to the art gallery, the museum, write a restaurant review.

Would you like to add some?

You can add five things to this list that are specific to you. Quilt, weave some tapestry, go for a run, shoot some hoops, walk the dog.

1. _____

2. _____

3. _____

4. _____

5. _____

I'll close up this section with something repetitious. Maybe you'll hear it this time. The fastest and easiest way to reset your mood is to sleep. Sleep cures a lot of what ails us: overwhelm, anxiety, agitation. A tiny nap is huge.

I still do this. I still hide in bed. Often. Regularly. When overwhelmed. When I want to pull the blanket up over my head. When I want to change the channel.

~~~~~~~~~~

Resource:

Audio ~ Sober Podcast 017: Sleep & Changing the Channel (how to change your mood), www.100daysoberchallenge.com/SP017

12. SUPPORT

When it was just me, alone in my head, I couldn't get more than nine days sober. Before I found the whole world of sober support, I kept falling into the wily traps of Wolfie. He'd say things like "you're going to fail later, might as well drink now." And then I would.

I would try again, read something, write something, and then drink. It took me a long time to reach out for some support. I swirled around for months. I tried to *will* myself to be sober. I thought I needed to 'try harder'.

We suck at getting support for being sober. This is a trait that we have in common. As a group, over-drinkers—you and me—we are sippers. Not as far as alcohol is concerned (clearly), but with respect to support.

We sip from the straw of support. There's a universe of support ideas, tools, and strategies. We sip. There are people around us who could be our sober cheerleaders. We hide. There's a smorgasbord of audios and downloads and groups and forums and counsellors and medications and treatment options.

And yet we nibble.

We don't want to reach out for help. It's embarrassing. *I don't deserve help. I just have to try harder.* If someone makes a gesture—to babysit, to share the work, we say "I'm fine." We're not fine. We're over-drinking and need help to quit. It's not weird or unusual to need tools and some supports: It's normal.

If you were learning to run, you would be open to support of all kinds: books, audios, coaches, groups, online buddies. Here is what you would NOT do. You would NOT decide to teach yourself to run with no reading, no tools. You would NOT head outside wearing a bathing suit and snow boots, totally ill-equipped. You would NOT run to the corner, fall over, and then go back home and say "I just need to try harder."

And yet, that's how we quit drinking. We start off, having no idea what to expect, we don't ask anyone who has done it before, we don't experiment with different tools. There is shame. We feel that we SHOULD be able to do this alone.

But there you are, in your bathing suit and your snow boots. You declare that today is a new Day 1 and off you go. Through some sheer force of will you perhaps get to the second corner before you fall over, again.

Here's how it could go. You could have someone tell you what to expect. You could read about the terrain ahead and what to avoid. You could carefully change out of your bathing suit and put on more appropriate clothes. You could go out slowly, doing a bit at a time, checking in with someone, asking for advice, listening to counsel, trusting people who have done it before. You could reward yourself for getting to the first corner, to the second corner.

Do you ask your shitty ex-best friend to be your cheerleader? No. Is your husband magically going to know what you need? No. You ask someone who's done it before. Who knows what it's like to be you. It's very common to turn to the person closest to you and expect that they can be your sober coach. And then they are no help. And then you think that you're a sucky failure.

If you feel like that, perhaps you have been asking the wrong people. There are people in your life who are wet blankets. They don't think your plans will work, no matter what they are. They don't understand what you're dealing with. They project their fears, worries, and shit onto you.

There are husbands who don't know what to say. There are wives who have loud Wolfies of their own who tell you that you're ruining the one good thing that you share (alcohol). There are counsellors who suggest that you're being too black and white, and that what you need is to learn to moderate. There are people who think you're 'fine' and that you don't have a problem, and then that makes you question what you're feeling.

And you, since you want to be sober, you turn and face someone else. I know this will make sense to you now, but the best person to help you run a marathon is someone who's done it before. And the best person to help you be sober, is another sober human.

Can you do it alone in your head? Probably not. Most of us make large changes in our lives through relation-ships with other people. When you are training to be an accountant, you have teachers. They don't drop off a box of books at your front door and ask you to figure it out yourself. You need to ask questions. That's how we learn.

If you're an introvert, or if you're a non-joiner like I am, then asking for any kind of support or encouragement seems hard. But here's the truth. The simple act of reaching out might make you feel weak, but it's actually a sign of strength.

Even in a teeny, tiny way, sending an email can make a difference. It can begin to tell your brain that you mean business, and that you're going to bring in reinforcements.

TRY THIS. I've just made up a newsletter called "Ideas On How to be Sober." It's a paper thing. Not electronic. Something you can carry around with you. Reread. Physically hold in your hands.

I'd like to send this newsletter to you in the mail. You do the teeny reaching out by sending a message using this special link: **www.100daysoberchallenge.com/iwantmail**

You can say: "Belle, I'd like to be sober but I don't know where to start. I'm freaked out. Can you send me a list of ideas on being sober?" Of course you can write what you like, this is just an idea.

Envelope from me will be plain, nothing weird. Nice colourful French stamps.

Your eyes will scan back and read that again, and you'll think "she gets too many messages, she won't read it, I can't tell anyone, this won't help." Your brain will say shit like that. Send the message anyway.

There are probably 60 individual sober tools and supports that we can use to help us be sober, from "go to bed early" all the way to up to inpatient rehab (you can find my list in the Appendix).

But we dabble. We try a few of the 60 things and then if we relapse, we usually try using the exact same very few supports and tools as the first time.

Imagine what would change if you did 20 or 30 things. And you did them all at once.

You'd have some sober momentum.

You'd feel better.

---

from Red: "Belle, here are my sober supports: You, my therapist, and my husband."

me: My lovely, you may find that sober support isn't just found in people. Don't forget all of the ways we remind ourselves that being sober is a good idea. Like reading blogs, having a sober penpal, going to bed early, taking medication, going to meetings, having a counsellor, ordering takeout, going for a run, crying, having a sober treat, listening to a sober podcast . . .

---

13. FOCUS ON WHAT YOU GET

Are you the type to feel rebellious, and say "Why can't I drink? Other people can drink. I feel so pissed off that I am giving up alcohol." This may describe you, it definitely described me. Turns out that the pouting, and the "why can't I drink" ideas come from focussing on not being ABLE to drink.

When you flip that idea of NOT BEING ABLE TO DRINK on its head, you can turn it into a decision that sounds like this:

"I don't drink because it's not good for me. I don't do cocaine either. There's a whole list of things I don't ingest because other people do. I do what's best for me. I also don't drive without a seat belt and I don't walk in dog shit. I am taking care of me."

You don't know what *normal* is any more. Alcohol has been affecting every single aspect of your life without you realizing it: when you go to bed, how much you eat, how you take vacations, how many vacations you can afford. Booze affects your bank account, your relationships, your sex life, your weight.

Then you take the alcohol away, and every bloody day is like waiting for a new normal. It often feels new, exciting, strange, and unusual.

Now, new and unusual does NOT mean that it is bad or that it is not working. It's just strange. You haven't done this before. You haven't had shitty days or celebrations without the accompanying three glasses of wine. So yes, to begin, there is some weirdness.

from Marsha (day 11): "I feel like a piece of raw meat but it's better than being in the hellacious cycle."

Wolfie will focus on the 20% that is hard, and may well ignore the good parts of being sober. When Wolfie says that being sober sucks and that it's too much to give up, you can remind him that you are also giving up the following:

- feeling like death in the morning
- waking at 3 a.m. with guilt and dread and horror
- vomiting
- spending dumb money (like money spent in bars, expensive bottles of wine in restaurants, buying rounds for people, impulse shopping online)
- emailing and texting random people
- hooking up with random people
- falling down
- hiding bottles
- arguing with your partner
- alternating stores so they don't get to know you
- cringing when it's time to take out the recycling

And here are a few of the things that you can focus on instead, the things you GET by being sober:

- you sleep through the night
- your skin looks great
- your health improves

- your marriage improves
- your kids talk to you again
- your family will now take your calls after 6 p.m.
- you can drive the car in the evening
- you have the beginnings of a hobby
- you can read a book and remember it
- you can watch a movie and stay awake for it
- you can actually cook the food in your fridge instead of eating popcorn for dinner
- you lift your head, look around, and feel like things are 'possible'
- you feel proud of yourself

There is a choice in how you see this, how you focus, what you tell yourself. If over-drinking is about weird and illogical thinking, then we have to learn to think in a new way. Old thinking: "I deserve this drink, one won't hurt, other people drink, why can't I be normal."

The Wolfie radio station broadcasts the same stuff to you and to me. You may hear something like: "I was a good girl, I used to be able to drink, I overdid it, now I'm being punished by having to give up booze entirely, it's like I'm a child standing in the corner. Everyone else is having fun now, except me."

Or you'll hear: "That woman on the patio drinking wine, she shines and sparkles, why can *she* have wine at three in the afternoon and I can't.

You have a choice. You can focus on the 20% hard part of being sober—the illusion of missed fun, the perceived 'good times' spent drunk on vacation—or you can focus on the 80% that is better.

Focus on what you get.

---

from Lou (day 16): "Today as I left work at 7 p.m. I saw a woman out on a sunny street drinking a glass of white. I need to remember the truly tedious discussions that would broadcast in my head at 4 a.m. if I took a leaf out of her book."

me: The other thing we don't consider when we see a woman like that, with her wine—we don't consider that it's her 6th glass, that maybe she's been secretly drinking all day at work. Or that she's going to drive after she finishes that 4th glass. We see what we think is romance, but we don't consider what happens before or after.

14. EVERYTHING ELSE IS WOLFIE

Winding yourself up? Wolfie. Taking on too much so that you feel wound up? Wolfie. Up at 4 a.m. working on Christmas presents to be opened the following morning? Wolfie. Skipping your morning ritual of sober reading, journaling, listening to audios, reaching out? Wolfie.

Any voice in your head that isn't saying 'take good care of you' is Wolfie.

But Belle, I can't tell if that voice is Wolfie or if it's me. I feel like such a slug. Shouldn't I be doing more? Wolfie.

You are doing more. You're being sober. Do you know what a big thing that is? Apparently not. Let me tell you.

You being sober is the foundation. It's the keystone habit. It's the thing that makes other things 'possible'. You being sober means that you'll be able to do those things in your head. Those dreams you have. The job change, the grad school, the renovation, the bakery, the movie. Raise your kids, train your dogs, blow your glass beads, bend your wire sculpture.

Being sober opens up dreams. You learn to count on yourself. It's easier to make long-term plans.

You drinking? On the couch in front of the TV (at best). On the street (at worst).

You say: Maybe my neighbour does aspire to drink 10 beers and watch reruns. Night after night after night.

I say: Wolfie. Do you think that your neighbour wants that to be her life? She's stuck in a place of listening to Wolfie, so much so that she's confused what is HER with what is booze. (I'm doing this because it's easier to see this with clarity when I talk about someone else. Look at her. Can you see her? She's in a nice middle-class home, upstairs in her girl-cave. Watching something crappy on TV.)

Yes, it's possible that your neighbour doesn't *want* to make a movie. It's possible that she isn't raising kids. It's also entirely possible that she doesn't want to train a dog unless she's training it to run far, far away and never come back.

But the voice in your head that says: just one beer, then I'll start the dishes is Wolfie. Just one more bad TV show then I'll go to bed. Wolfie. I'll quit drinking on Monday. After this next work thing. After the niece's birthday party. After the holidays. Wolfie.

The voice that says maybe a bath first, then bed. That's you.

I deserve a cup of mint tea. You. Wonder what I could make with that yarn if I unravelled that sweater with the forest green wool and started again. You.

If I start now I can make a three-course dinner, do the dishes, clean the floor on my hands and knees, why isn't anybody helping me, make some lunches, and then iron my clothes for tomorrow. Wolfie.

But wait, Belle, maybe she does have to do all those things?

No, she doesn't. But Wolfie will say she does.

Does she *need* to make a three-course dinner? No. Do the dishes (despite popular belief, they CAN wait until morning), clean the floor (there are children for these tasks, and if not children, then dogs), why isn't anybody helping? Because you're taking on too much and whipping yourself into a frenzy, and so everyone is Keeping a Wide Berth from you and your nuttiness; make some lunches (those kids can make their own lunches, or you can make simpler lunches that don't involve homemade applesauce started at 10 p.m.); you can take your clothes to the cleaners, you can get a shirt washed and ironed for like two bucks.

But I don't want to do it your way. I need to do all those things.

I know it feels that way. That's Wolfie. The voice that winds you up, that makes drinking seem like a good idea.

And you? You're learning this. You're learning it now.

TRY THIS. Sometimes it's easier to hear a message in an audio. I've made up a one minute message for you and I really think you should stop and listen to it now.

Audio ~ One Minute 006: Foundation,
www.100daysoberchallenge.com/foundation

PART 3.

THE 100-DAY SOBER CHALLENGE

OK, SO YOU'VE DONE ALL OF THE RESEARCH. You have read about being sober. You have some idea what to expect. So here you are, sitting in your little sober car on the side of the road, ready to begin. You put your hands firmly on 10-and-2, and you have someone sitting beside you, pointing out the big speed bumps and helping to navigate your sober car into the correct lane.

There is a certain amount of concentration that is required in the beginning that will ease off as you go along. Like learning to drive, you start with your senses on high alert and feel some unease because everything is new. Then eventually you are driving along, you have momentum, you can listen to the radio. You slow down in bad weather, you put fuel in your sober car, and you keep going no matter what.*

----

* You can find the entire blog post "Sobriety is like a little car" here **www.100daysoberchallenge.com/car**. Make sure to check the truly hilarious comments from Facingfacts about Samuel L. Jackson and Stevie Wonder and how it relates to being newly sober. There's also a more lyrical description of the sober car on Medium, here **www.100daysoberchallenge.com/sobercar**

Here is your sober pledge:

"I will not drink for 100 days. No matter what. I can cry, but I will not drink. I can go to bed or go home early. I might feel distressed, but I will not drink. Bad things might happen, but I will not drink. Incredibly shitty things may happen to someone around me, or my neighbour, or my friend's friend's grandmother. But there will be no booze. Funerals? Weddings? Amputation? I'm not drinking for 100 days no matter what happens. No matter what."

You can write a copy of the pledge and do it longhand with a pen and a piece of paper. Make a note of your last drink. Carry this piece of paper in your wallet, or laminate it, or stick it under a magnet on the fridge.

KEEP A JOURNAL.

Before I outline the timeline of the 100-Day Sober Challenge, I will stop now to encourage you to keep a short journal of your own, particularly for the first 60 days. I know you don't want to do this, but it will be helpful I promise. For example, if you're on Day 51 and having a particularly difficult day, it'll be helpful for you to flip back to an earlier day to see that you were feeling proud of yourself. Not every day feels like progress, but when you read your writing, you will see sober momentum building up as you conquer more days. Just because you can't see the grass growing, doesn't mean it's not happening. How's that for a sentence with a whole lot of negatives.

By keeping a daily record you can see the grass grow. And you can more clearly identify that some periods of time are shitty but that they don't last, and they're followed swiftly by easier days.

For example, here's an extract from my blog from when I was on Day 19:

No explanation, no justification

I didn't try to 'hide' that I wasn't drinking. In fact, at dinner, while everyone else enjoyed the homemade cocktails, the champagne, the wine, and the liqueur that I had on the table, I made a big pot of tea and put it next to my plate, and over the course of the evening I proceeded to drink the entire pot. Not one single person gave a shit, except mr-lonely-drinker-why-do-you-have-to-be-my-mirror. OK so I guess I'm still gloating. Good morning Day 19. I've never been here before :)

~~~~~

Source: Blog post, www.100daysoberchallenge.com/noexplanation

---

Then Day 51 was a surprisingly shitty day for me, and I wanted to quit the whole sober thing:

The end of an experiment

I am going to end my sober experiment at the end of the month. I am not planning to drink that day, and I'm not going to return to drinking every day, but I'm tired of this. Like, supremely tired. Yes, the wolf is getting quieter and quieter. Yes it's getting easier. But to what point? I've lost the plot now.

~~~~~

Source: Blog post, www.100daysoberchallenge.com/experiment

Moods can fluctuate, and when I was having that crap day, it really helped to be able to look back and review that just a short while before I thought that being sober was *glorious*. It helped to remind me that some days are just randomly odd.

If you want to follow along with where I was day by day, you can read my blog in order either online or in the collected PDF.

Like the pregnancy book, *What to Expect When You're Expecting*, we want to flip through page by page, and read about what is happening to us and what we can expect. We want clarification on "how long will *this* phase last?"

While you will not have the exact same trajectory that I did (we are different sober humans after all), I *have* been sober penpals with 2,400+ people, and what I describe here is an entirely unscientific yet pretty accurate map of what you might expect.

WHAT TO EXPECT: DAY 1.

You drank last night, you went to bed, you woke up today on your first sober day.* You don't know what to expect but you're braced for Day 1 to be a shit day. Not gigantically terrible, but not glorious either. You may feel exhausted and hungover. You may feel relieved.

The morning of Day 1 is a good time to make a list. You can start your journal with this entry. Start with a list of 10 things:

1. The way I drink has affected my _____

2. And my _____

3. And my _____

4. It's caused problems with _____

5. And _____

6. It's made me feel _____ especially

   when _____

---

* Again, I'll put in the disclaimer here about getting medically supervised detox if you require it. Not everyone can abruptly stop drinking. Be sensible about this.

7. I nearly had a disaster when _____

8. And this was just about a disaster too: _____

_____

9. I'm tired of waking up feeling like _____

10. People who will be relieved that I am sober:

_____

_____

_____

_____

For question #10 above, you can start with your spouse, children, coworkers, parents, neighbours, friends, siblings, roommates. You might actually have 100 people around you whose lives are affected by what you do. For example, it's not only your adult daughter, but her husband and her children and her in-laws. I know you don't think your drinking is (or could become) important to others. You'd be wrong. Maybe you're single, you have a lousy job, and you hardly talk to your mother. It doesn't matter. The people around you are still affected by you. If you die tomorrow by passing out drunk in the bathtub

(I've nearly done this, it's not as unlikely as you might think), then for a moment try to imagine who would be saddened that you died. Who would say they didn't know you were over-drinking, only that you didn't seem happy or like yourself? Who would say that your death affected them, their relationships, or their ability to connect with others going forward? Who would feel terrible that they didn't know you weren't able to quit drinking for any length of time, and that you never asked for help? Imagine who would feel shitty that they didn't try to speak to you about your drinking, those who knew you were struggling, but it never seemed like the right time to say anything, and they were afraid of your reaction.

While your list probably does include 100 people, you can start with 10. Or 30. I'll wait. You can continue your list from above here:

_____

_____

_____

_____

_____

_____

Now write yourself a postcard, a small summary, 4–5 sentences maximum:

Dear Me: I want to remember the feeling of how bad it is to be hungover. I'm going to write a few sentences here that I can reread later when I (might) think that drinking would be a good idea. I never want to feel like this again:

_____

_____

_____

_____

_____

_____

_____

_____

On Day 1, you get your replacement drinks (flip back to the section on replacement drinks in Part 2 if you need a refresher). Plan your dinner for tonight and tomorrow night. Have a sober treat every two days, or every day if you're feeling particularly shitty. Go to bed fully clothed if Wolfie acts up. Watch bad TV and do not allow yourself to feel guilty. And you will (really) go to sleep as early as you can manage it.

This is the first of your email check-ins.

I've created a special email address where you can send your sober progress. *The act of sending messages to the sober universe can really help* so don't skip this step. Remember the section at the beginning of this book where I said I was going to ask you to try some things that you would think didn't work—and that you were going to try them anyway? This is one of those things.#

OK, for your first email on Day 1, send a message to say that you are underway. You can attach a copy of what you just wrote above, or your message can simply say "Today is my Day 1." Use this special email address: **email@100daysoberchallenge.com**

Don't discount the usefulness of sending a message even if you do not get a personalized response. Your brain appreciates that you are reaching out, and the act of reaching out shifts how you feel. That said, if you would like to have a real sober penpal, and receive replies to your emails, and have me keep track of your sober days, then read more here: **www.soberjumpstart.com**. The email address above, though, is free for anyone to use. It's just a one-way channel instead of a two-way communication.

THE FIRST WEEK SOBER, DAYS 2-7.

Your baby is the size of a peanut (OK, wrong book). You wake on Day 2 and you are relieved. *Thank god, no hangover, didn't drink last night, wow the mornings are so great.* You may even roll over, wait to feel terrible, and then feel immensely grateful that you do not have to scroll through your memory of "what happened, what did I do?" You don't have to check your sent email to see what kind of mischief took place last night.

For the first week or so, physically you may feel intermittently unwell, like you have the flu (see the section on "feeling shitty for the first week"). Symptoms may include headache, fatigue, an unfocussed brain, and moods that range from irritated to bored to weepy.

If you actually pretend that you *have* the flu, then you will do flu-taking-care-of-you things. You'll drink water, watch television, order take-out, sleep as much as you can, and do as little at work as possible to not get fired. Laundry can wait. What? You always do the laundry every day? Imagine that you're sick. You wouldn't do the laundry. You wouldn't cook dinner.

---

from A: "Why should being sober for the first week be so hard? I should just suck it up, why be such a baby about it?"

Here's the truth. Your poor body needs to adjust to weeks and years where you poured booze on your head as the solution to *all* of life's problems. So yes, it takes time for your physical-ness to recover. I've read that it can take up to nine days for the alcohol to fully leave your system. During this time, you may feel fatigued, or like you're sick, or like you have a headache.

Imagine this. You were in the hospital for a routine procedure, like having your appendix removed. Once you get home, you would take some time to recover.

I know, you think it's ridiculous that I'm spelling out 'self-care' like this. But after weeks and years of over-drinking, you have probably forgotten (I had) what self-care looks like. It's not a 'touchy-feely getting aligned with the planets' thing. It's a 'listening to your insides, figuring out what you need' thing. And when we're drinking we don't do this—at all. We lose touch entirely with what our body needs. We are dazed, skip meals, anaesthetize ourselves to the point of not feeling much of anything. We keep drinking when we don't feel good. We wake up feeling like a shit stain. We vomit or fall down or drive or heave or cry or apologize.

None of that is self-care. It just isn't.

So yes, the first week sober, you are adjusting to a world without alcohol, both mentally and physically. The physical part often feels like the flu. Is that normal? Yes. Does it go away? Yes. What should you do? Pretend you have the flu and do flu-taking-care-of-you kinds of things.

I've said this enough. You get it, right?

Email when you are on Day 7 and share how you're feeling
physically, and what you are doing to help yourself feel better.
What kinds of self-care things are you doing, even if you don't
think they're working, even if you feel gigantically gross.

Use this special email address: **email@100daysoberchallenge.com**

This first week sober is probably the weirdest in the
whole 100-Day Sober Challenge. Your mood and emotions may well be all over the place. Gloriously gloating
at your sober rock star status, and then ten minutes later
crashing into 'how will I be able to do this?'

All normal.

You'll make dinner for a while until it feels too strange,
then you'll read some sober blogs. Your mood will shift.
You'll put a sober podcast on the headphones, and then
return to chopping onions for vegetarian chili.

CHANGE YOUR ROUTINE.

Once you're through the first week, you might worry
that the weekend will be harder. I have a newsflash for
you. Fridays are just another day of the week. They don't
'mean' drinking, despite what your brain may tell you.

Our brains are used to doing things a certain way, mostly on autopilot. We come in the front door, open the wine, start drinking. It seems to happen without thought.

When you first quit drinking, you will have to think about what you are doing, and when. It will help to make new patterns if you shuffle your schedule around. For example, go to the gym mid-afternoon, or go for a walk at 6 p.m. You can feed the kids earlier, and then listen to a sober podcast and eat later. You could have a bath during your usual dinner time.

---

from DC: "I drove to the city today and a part of my routine [on Fridays] is to have some beer after work to take the edge off of things. I am working on a plan today that totally changes my approach to heading home and drinking. I'm grateful for you. Thanks so much, DC"

me: Smart move, if you change your routine you're more likely to be successful. Also, if you eat pancakes/breakfast for dinner, you're less likely to drink :)

DC: "Oh my gosh, that may be the funniest advice I've ever gotten. Pancakes it is. That is hilarious!! Thank you!!"

me: Have a nice hot chocolate. And then say "Fuck You Wolfie. I'm in charge of me."

DC: "Oh, Belle, thank you. I just stopped by a Cracker Barrel and had pancakes and hot chocolate for dinner. I'm grateful for you!! Hugs back at ya!"

DAY 16 IS A TURNING POINT.

While Day 14 is great (hooray, two weeks, cake, parades), there is something special that begins around Day 16. You're far enough away from Day 1 that you feel like you have some momentum (and you do). It's close enough to Day 30 that you can see that milestone coming up (a month, a whole month, holy cowie).

[You may have a good 'turning point day' on Day 15 or on Day 17, or earlier or later, but it is usually right around here. This isn't science; this is based on my 176,965 emails back and forth with sober penpals (yes, that's a real number that I just checked while writing this note to you on Feb. 26, 2016). My sober penpals often get tense if things don't work out EXACTLY. So I'll just step in here to say this: Do not get weird about the specifics. We have a tendency to be granular and particular and obsessive, and to think that it isn't working for us. If you are sober, and you are on Day 16, then it *is* working for you.]

Daisies and sunshine rocketing out of my ass

It hasn't all been daisies and sunshine rocketing out of my ass, BUT I have been collecting ideas, and I've been discovering NEW thoughts that I can feed into my logic loop. Instead of mulling over: "eventually I'm going to drink," I've now replaced that kind of thinking with "I like this stillness and quiet-headed-ness, and I'm so glad I have time to take care of the REST of my life" . . . I thus happily begin Day 16 knowing that I will not drink today :)

~~~~~

Source: Blog post, www.100daysoberchallenge.com/daisies

Email when you are on Day 16 to report the turning-point-ness of the day. How does it feel compared to Day 1? How proud are you of what you've done so far (not proud enough, freaked out, very proud, elated, shocked, amazed)?

Use this special email address: **email@100daysoberchallenge.com**

As the rest of the first month rolls along, each day is incrementally easier. If the worst of the physical symptoms are done by Day 7–9, and Day 16 is a turning point, then what is there to look forward to on the downhill slope to Day 30?

Sober sleep. You remember sleeping through the night, don't you? You may not. When I was drinking—no matter what quantity—I'd routinely wake up in the middle of the night and fret and toss around for some length of time, hot and irritated, often with a depressed sense that I was absolutely going to quit drinking 'tomorrow'.

And then when I first quit drinking, I was routinely sleeping 12 hours a night. I had a lot of naps. I slept a lot. You probably will, too. Yes, it's normal. And glorious. You don't remember what it's like to sleep through the night? You're going to love it.

DAY 30 IS A GOOD REASON TO CELEBRATE.

So here you are on Day 30. You're sleeping better. You have your own top 10 reasons why it's been good to be sober. You have a sober treat planned to celebrate (ice cream, fireworks, glitter). It's a big milestone. Being sober is a big deal. It's hard, and you're doing it. Hooray for you :)

You will probably feel pretty darn proud of yourself. You may also notice that no one around you notices, celebrates, or gives a shit. If your husband doesn't have a Wolfie voice, he doesn't know what you're doing, or how hard it is. Most of your supportive friends won't get it either. But do you know who gets it? Another sober person. If you start to feel disappointed that no one bought you a blue Volvo station wagon to celebrate your 30th sober day (don't they realize how hard this is?), then you can turn and face the sober world. There are many of us here. We will send you virtual Volvos. And hugs. And we can confirm your rock star status.

You knew I was going to say this: You will definitely *get yourself* a treat to celebrate 30 Days. You can take care of you and plan the reward, plan the event, get the cake, have the day off. You can do the thing for you, yourself. And you should.

Ten good reasons to be 30 days sober:

1. Celebrating a new 'personal best' every day. That doesn't happen much when you're an adult, taking on a new skill and seeing progress and improvement each and every day.

2. Sleeping through the night. My doctor thought I was pre-menopausal when I complained of waking at 4 a.m. She should have asked how many glasses of wine I was having every night (answer: 3+).

3. No arguments. I haven't had one disagreement with my husband in 30 days. I can't tell you how often I used to go to bed teary, feeling completely misunderstood. That seems to be over.

4. Supportive sober (online) friends.

5. No one gives a shit that I'm not drinking. All the worries of not 'fitting in' or being 'different' if I gave up drinking were totally bogus. No one gives a rat's ass. I drink tea and you drink wine? Who cares. We go to dinner, you guys order wine, I say *I'm not drinking*, only one comment in 30 days from a social acquaintance I see about every six weeks, and now will see even less.

6. It is quiet(er) in my head. This is the main reason I have given up drinking . . . I drank much more than I wanted to, didn't seem to be able to string together many days alcohol-free. I used to spend a lot of time thinking about when I could drink, how much, was there enough, should I start drinking from my husband's glass when he left the room.

7. I'm a nicer person. I'm kinder and more patient and less sarcastic. Much less sarcastic. I think I see people more clearly now.

8. My irritation and frustration levels are diminished. This is a side by-product of being sober that I did not anticipate. Didn't realize that drinking made me really grumpy, and itchy in my own skin. I think I'm less impulsive, too. Certainly there've been NO late-night stupid emails (to friends and clients) promising the moon.

9. Motivation levels are higher. I used to get a lot done before. Now I'm getting things done *with purpose*. I'm not running all over town on some kind of 'urgent' mission. Now I make plans and cross things off the list.

10. I've stopped straightening my hair. OK, you can laugh if you want to. But straight hair is all the rage, and for the last 30 days I've just stopped. (Honestly some days it takes all of my concentration and focus to get up and get through the day, remember to run, to eat 3 times a day, and to not-drink.) I have naturally curly hair that I've been forcing into 'style' with a hot iron. This has stopped . . . I think it's also an outward expression of being more comfortable in my own skin. Or it shows a complete abandon of personal grooming while I focus hard on being sober. We'll see.

I feel I should now re-order the list, to end with something punchy and strong. Instead it ends with a vain comment about my hair. Oh well, there you go. I have cute curly hair, that isn't the least bit in style. I'll keep you posted.

~~~~~

Source: Blog post, www.100daysoberchallenge.com/30days

Email when you are on Day 30 to say how you are sleeping. Has it improved since Day 1? Do you still wake at 4 a.m. with dread and panic? Don't forget to mention how you are celebrating your Day 30 (daytime movie, trip to bakery, new fuzzy socks, burger take-out, afternoon in the park).

Use this special email address: **email@100daysoberchallenge.com**

DAY 42, YOU FEEL BRAVER.

If you've been staying pretty close to home, then you'll notice that right around the 6-week mark you begin to feel braver. You might meet a friend for lunch and order Perrier. Maybe you drop into an after-work event, grab a glass of tonic, smile, and then exit.

There is no rush with this out-in-the-world-social-izing step. You will know when it's time, and you'll do more of it when you feel up to it. Do not email and say that you are turning into a hermit! There is no right-timing on this, except to say that the further away from Day 1 you get, the better you feel. And usually around the 6-week mark you feel *less* wobbly, and slightly *more* able to cope in social settings. As you learn to be more resilient, the idea of a potluck at your neighbours' doesn't seem as impossible as it did to you on Day 1.

Often penpals tell me that they don't feel up to going to some event. And my response, predictably, reliably, which I say so often that I have a macro for it in my email, is this:

> **me:** *I probably didn't socialize outside the home more than 2–3 times in the first 6 weeks sober. I just felt safer at home with my tea and my routines. Take good care of you.*

DAY 50, AND I DO LOVE A HALF-WAY POINT.

When I do a long run, I love the 'turn around point' because then it's all downhill in my mind. In the second half, I don't have to check my watch, I run until I'm home again. The second half goes by more quickly.

There are a lot of similarities between running and being sober. On long runs, I often feel like a bag of shit for the first half, and I have now learned that that's normal for me. I know to *keep going* through the crappy part, and then I feel better. I have learned (the hard way) to never quit during the first part, just wait, it improves—and it always does. If I stop and have to start again, I beat myself up; it's easier to keep going.

The same with being sober. Any shitty sober day is better than a new Day 1. The first half may drag in terms of time, it'll seem like forever to get to Day 50, and then you wake up one day and it's easier. You turn and you can see Day 100 coming up, over the horizon, around the corner, it's a few stops along the highway in your sober car.

DAY 60, TWO MONTHS, LET THERE BE ANGELS AND CANDLES.

I don't want to make it sound easy or without challenges, but the second month sober is much easier than the first. You've figured some things out. You're more comfortable telling people about your "self-discipline challenge" (*see the upcoming section on who to tell and what to say*). You will feel dramatically better than you did that first week sober. If you want to check, you can reread what you wrote on the morning of Day 1.

Be very proud of Day 60. There are a million people (at least) who wish they were here with you now. Day 60 is two whole months of saying no to Wolfie, 60 glorious bricks in the wall between Day 1 and now. You're glad month one is done. You're relieved that month two was easier. You've got sober momentum.

The other thing that happens right around Day 60 is the thinking about NOT drinking virtually stops. The witching hour has mostly faded. You don't have to consciously NOT drink. You'll have whole individual days where you don't think about drinking at all. You will email me and say: "you said it would happen, but I didn't believe it would happen FOR ME. But I have to tell you, I didn't think about drinking today. The voice is finally quiet. Oh my god I never thought this day would arrive."

In fact, you should email on Day 60. Tell the sober universe that you have arrived in your sober car at a town called "Sober is the New Normal." And make sure to include the part where you were *sure* it wouldn't happen for you—until it did.

Use this special email address: **email@100daysoberchallenge.com**

DAY 90 IS MORE OF THE SAME, BUT BETTER.

You feel lighter. Your face is less puffy. You sleep better. You're strangely more patient. You're less irritated with your idiot co-workers. You can see your child's melt-down as an expression of exhaustion rather than a plot to drive you insane. You often feel 'pink clouds' which are gloriously high, elated, *fuck I am really doing this*, feelings. Pink clouds get bad press in the sober media, but don't be fooled. They're great. You feel like (finally!) you're taking care of yourself, you're feeling better all the time, you're sure that THIS is the thing that all the sober people blog about when they say "keep going, it gets better."

DAY 95, AND IT'S TIME FOR A NEW PLAN.

Wolfie likes to act up around soberversaries, so when you arrive at the town called Day 95, it's a good time to get out your map and choose your next goal. I suggest Day 180, because if Day 100 is great, then Day 180 is something else entirely. Not only do you feel better on Day 180 BUT you can look up, look around, see where you've come from AND where you're going. It's like arriving on a hill and having a fantastic clear view ahead. So if you feel weird around Day 95, which is how I always feel right when I'm about to complete a goal, then you make a new goal. And you plan your Day 100 treat. Go and do it right now. Put something into your Amazon shopping cart. Don't skip this step.

DAY 100 IS SUCCESSFULLY ACHIEVING YOUR FIRST GOAL.

You are light years away from where you were on Day 1. Things that you didn't think you would survive have happened. You are proud of yourself. You're relieved. You recognize that not all of life's problems are solved, but that by being sober, solving problems becomes *possible*.

You may not believe me. You might believe these folks. Here are some Day 100 emails from my sober penpals:

> **from Lavenderzone (Day 100):** "I want to give you my sincere thanks for all that you have done for me. I was never able to do this before and now I have a completely different life—thank god! I have learned a lot of things along the way that work well for me (treats, staying busy, developing my passions and going to bed if all else fails). Wolfie doesn't say much these days and I nudge him away from my thoughts like a little lightweight whiff of Kleenex when he does. What a difference from 100 days ago—you were and are so right . . . I feel strong, alive and quite happy and not interested in alcohol at all." [Update: She's on day 165 today.]

from Silverbirch (Day 100): "Do you know what? I actually AM feeling better about the whole thing, particularly over these last few days. I feel less 'deprived' than before, and am starting to feel that I am choosing not to drink, rather than that I'm depriving myself of something desirable. I'm starting to be able to see alcohol for the false friend that it was, one of these toxic friends that you're better off without. We went to friends' for dinner last night, and probably for the first time since I've started this journey, I didn't feel envious or deprived. In fact, I realize I wasn't thinking about drinking much at all—I was trying to moderate the amount of sugary elderflower fizz I was drinking (it was lovely!) and looking forward to the food. It was only later on I realized that I hadn't felt bitter about 'denying' myself, and that the not drinking hadn't been the focus of my evening. You have consistently reassured me that it gets easier when you're at 100+ days and I'm hoping I'm now getting to that stage..." [Update: She's on Day 257 today.]

from Carrie (Day 100): "Wow, I can't believe it. I am so happy to be writing this email. I cannot thank you enough for being my sober friend and for the 100-Day Sober Challenge idea, both of which have helped me get to this momentous day. I can't believe that I have been sober for this long and have plans only to stay sober and happy too!

I made a million promises to myself that I would cut down or give up booze. I needed to do something differently this time as my attempts always failed in the end. *I would always convince myself that I had probably just overreacted and back to drinking I would go!* I needed to admit to someone other than myself that I needed help. I needed to be understood. I needed someone to empathise with my situation and most of all, I needed to be accountable.

The sober challenge and the online sober community gave my sobriety a whole new sense of purpose. It's not just about not drinking. It's about sharing fears, expressing feelings, asking for help, opening up, showing vulnerability and baring your soul. It's about being encouraged, receiving praise, cheers, shout outs! It's about giving advice too, supporting others, hoping, praying for them to do well. It's following their journey, rooting for them, cheering them on, keeping each other company on the good days and the bad. It's knowing someone has your back. Someone who understands.

Drinking and worrying about my drinking had taken over my life. I couldn't imagine a life without wine and yet I couldn't imagine how my life was going to continue if I was drinking so heavily. I am back in control and drinking doesn't dominate everything I do. Every decision doesn't revolve around obsessing about alcohol. It's an exciting, scary, new feeling but I would chose this over the constant thinking about alcohol every time.

Having 100 days has given me the strength to face 100 more. So I am going for 200 days sober, wow, I never thought I would say that!" [Update: She's on day 1083 today.]

Send an email to say you are on Day 100. You can say how you're feeling, what your plans are, and that you're signing up to extend to 180 days.

Use this special email address: **email@100daysoberchallenge.com**

PART 4. QUESTIONS

RIGHT WHEN YOU FIRST QUIT, there are a lot of questions, a lot of unknowns. Part of why we ALL struggle in the first few days sober is because it's all so new, so foreign to how we usually live.

Questions like: "Can I have fun if I don't drink? What will I tell my best friend? What does it mean if I have to start again on Day 1?"

And so on.

I often felt like if I didn't have the answer to a question IMMEDIATELY, that I'd explode. There's a pressure in the unknown. We hate being in the dark. That's you and me both.

Since the initial question-asking stage of sobriety is deafening, here are some of the questions you are going to ask along with some of my answers. These are all based on real emails in my inbox.

WHY DO I OVER-DRINK?

> **from Sha:** "Why did I always put alcohol over many other aspects of my life? Why can't I ever be satisfied with one or two drinks?

We want the answers before we start. We want to know the difference between drinking alcoholically and being an alcoholic. We want to know why we self-sabotage.

Here's my answer: Do the action first, stop trying to figure out why.

I mentioned this drinking logic loop before, but I'm sure that my perfectionism in thinking I had to figure out drinking FIRST, probably kept me from quitting drinking for a long time even though I knew I was drinking more than I should.

The perfectionist in me wanted to FIND A WAY TO KEEP DRINKING—not be so all or nothing about it, surely moderation should be possible if I find out HOW TO DO IT RIGHT.

(Lots of shouty caps, sorry.)

So. Quit drinking for a medium-longish length of time (100–180 days) and then figure out later if you feel better or worse once you're sober. Do you obsess less, do you sleep better, do you feel better, are you prouder of yourself?

That you can't imagine any of these things BEFORE you quit drinking doesn't mean anything. Begin. The clarity comes later. Says me, the behaviourist.

There'll be a therapist out there who will come to correct me, saying "you need to know the ROOT CAUSE before you can find a solution" and I'll call bullshit.

Because you cannot figure out drinking while you are still drinking.

Yes, events have happened in our past that drive our behaviour. That's a fact. But it's what we DO next that changes things.

A lot of time is spent standing around trying to understand. We think that our over-drinking is a logic problem that can be solved.

You don't want to quit and you want to know why. My answer is: "Doesn't matter. You don't have to want to quit. What you do have to want is to feel better than you feel now. You know the hungover, tired, deal-making, exhausting, hiding, exaggerating, lying, disappointed, spent feeling. Yeah that.

And maybe you've been pouring booze on your head for so long that you don't know what 'better' feels like. So then you have to do this sober thing on faith. Faith that those of us who are longer-term sober stay this way because we choose this. It feels better. It's plain easier.

That's hard to understand when you're drinking. But what if it was a challenge. What if you were challenged to quit drinking for some short, defined length of time, so you could see how much better things might be when the booze stops.

It doesn't matter what you THINK about quitting drinking.

Doesn't matter if you use the word alcoholic or not.

Doesn't matter if you want to quit forever.

Doesn't matter if you don't know why you drink.

Stop drinking for 100 days and THEN you'll start to figure out how you feel about it.

~~~~~~~~~~

Resource:

Blog post ~ Do you change the behaviour first?
www.100daysoberchallenge.com/behaviour

WILL I STILL HAVE FUN WHEN I'M SOBER?

> **from Liza (day 5):** "I'm worried about how I'll be in social situations such as get-togethers, and I enjoy going to see live music which is often at a bar. I still want to be able to have fun. I'm an introvert and not that much fun on my own."

It's entirely possible to have sober fun, of course it is :) Those of us who are longer-term sober have plenty of fun. There's nothing better than waking up without a hangover, without regret, without shame. There's nothing better than being on a beach and being sober and watching a sunset. There's nothing better than coming home at the end of a long night, or dancing until 4 a.m., knowing that you had a fabulous time, that you rocked it all without a drink.

To think that you need alcohol to have fun is Wolfie talking. You were fun when you were 12 years old. You've had hilarious pee-your-pants laughing with your best friend and it didn't involve alcohol. Wolfie tells you that kind of shit to encourage you to drink, but it's not true. Can you dance sober? Turns out you can. Who knew.

There's nothing better than sober fun because it's fun had with no cost. There are no repercussions the next day. You can have fun and skip the "oh my god what did they think of me, my husband is going to find out, my kid saw me throwing up again"—all of that stops. So if you're going to miss *something*, you can miss losing your keys, miss taking money out of the bank and then going back the same night and taking out more again. It isn't fun to fall or slip or trip. It isn't fun to be embarrassed and to have to call people and say "I'm sorry I know I texted you—I said something in front of your boyfriend—I made a pass at your wife."

If you go to a bar and there is a concert, you can have a nice time drinking tonic and watching the music. We often worry about how other people are going to see us, but it turns out that you with a glass of soda in your hands isn't that interesting. *No one sees or registers anything.* While our drinking is very important to *us*, it is not that important to other people.

Introverts have fun. Wolfie may tell you that every person on the planet who is having fun has consumed alcohol first. Not true. And the more time you spend in the sober community, the more you realize that there are whacks of us out here who are hilarious, entertaining, loud or quiet, and we're soberly-socializing with a tall glass of tonic and a smile on our faces. That's what I want for you.

~~~~~~~~~~

Resource:

Audio ~ Sober Podcast 020: Fun,
www.100daysoberchallenge.com/SP020

ISN'T REGULAR ALCOHOL CONSUMPTION SUPPOSED TO BE 'GOOD' FOR YOU?

from Sober in Richmond (day 255): "My biggest worry about being long term sober: is it healthy? I know this sounds crazy, but there have been many studies that say that alcohol in moderation is a good thing—especially for the heart. What if, years down the road, my doctor says, 'It might have been better for you had you drank alcohol in moderation. Your cholesterol is high and alcohol would have helped maintain that.' I'm not a doctor, so I don't know what the fuck I'm talking about. But you DID ask what's my biggest worry, and that's my biggest worry!" [Update: he's on day 414 today]

I hate these kinds of studies because I feel like they leave out important things. They are looking at alcohol as a plus/minus—what are the benefits with or without. But they don't look at what comes with alcohol.

If there was a mythical one glass of wine, then what comes with that? While it might improve heart health, with that glass of wine would come the following: skipping your after dinner work out, eating more generously, extra empty calories for no reason, and the likelihood of more alcohol later.

If you remove the alcohol, and you lose some tiny heart benefit, there are easier ways to improve your health with no downsides. Like exercise, and a reduced cholesterol diet.

So what I'm saying is that you can't look at alcohol as one thing. It's a whole murky package of things that don't quite add up.

I hear that cod liver oil is good for digestion, too.

I hear that toothpaste gives you cancer.

I hear that over-drinking for you and me is a bad idea, because it affects every other fucking part of our life—not just our heart. It affects our souls.

WHAT ABOUT MODERATION?

from Olson: "I am solidly committed to the 100 days and I feel good. I am still wondering about moderation versus abstinence in the future . . . There is no doubt in my mind that my prior drinking habits were bad for my mind and my body. And I'm 100% sure I don't want to go back there. Wondering if moderate drinking is salvageable for me . . . I would appreciate your advice."

I wish I could definitively answer, once and for all, the question: "Can I drink after 100 days?" I'd like to have a button I can push when I get this question by email that could give out a set answer.

But here's the thing, every person who asks the question is a different person. You have a different bottom, a different situation, you have kids, or don't, you have a supportive spouse, or don't—and every single person (without fail) is asking me the question (again), because they are *certain that their situation is different.*

I've been asked this question so many times it makes me want to cry because this is the typical result for those who decide to 'try' moderation: "Belle, I did the 100-Day Sober Challenge. I started drinking again. It's been 18 months. I can't get a new Day 1. Why did I start drinking again?"

People who can moderate—normal drinkers—are already doing it. They can have a drink or not, and they don't care.

If you're talking about *controlled drinking,* this is when we know we are drinking more than we want to, and we set up a series of rules for ourselves to follow to hopefully keep things contained.

Controlled drinking is not very successful—you know this already because you've tried it. If we have to control our drinking, it means that our natural, default tendency is to have one, and then another, and then another. Any plan we make is very difficult, if not impossible, to adhere to. It's not about whether we drink three glasses or three bottles a night: we start with the intention of drinking 'something', and we end up in a different place.

I will now give you my best sympathetic face, touch your arm, try to get you to look at me, and I'll say this:

You tried moderation. You did. You maybe didn't call it moderation. You tried making rules for yourself. When you realized that you were drinking more than you wanted to, before you ever saw this book, you did things like alternating every second glass with water, or switching from hard stuff to beer, or trying to skip days. You tried to drink only on weekends, or only have one, or only . . . or only . . . or only.

When we have one drink, we lose the ability to make other decisions about what happens next.

It's easier to have none.

~~~~~~~~~

Resources:

Audio ~ Sober Podcast 133: Drinking is not required,
www.100daysoberchallenge.com/required

Audio ~ One Minute Message 029: It's easier to have none,
www.100daysoberchallenge.com/none

Blog post ~ Drinking regret, www.100daysoberchallenge.com/regret

BUT BELLE, MY DOCTOR (COUNSELLOR, THERAPIST) THINKS I'M OVERREACTING.

If someone doesn't have a drinking issue, they don't realize the brain space that is occupied by booze. Once we finally get that noise to stop, then it's sort of silly for someone to suggest that we try to drink again. Why would we reintroduce the problem again, only to have to start all over on a new Day 1 later? If your doctor feels that you are 'not a real alcoholic'—who cares! Does that mean you should continue to drink? It's like doctors forget that no one NEEDS to drink. And if we're happier without it, then so be it.

Consider this email I received from JenniferKay, who was worried that her new therapist wasn't a good fit:

---

from JenniferKay: "I had my second therapy session today.

She said that we need to examine the reasons why I stopped drinking. She said that it was very black and white thinking. She said that I did not drink in excess. She said that online support people probably were drinking much more than me. She said that stopping drinking was a control issue.

Basically, she said that I need to journal about my reasons for not drinking and that I needed to be more confident about not drinking and giving specific reasons not to drink.

At my first appointment, I'd told her exactly the truth about how I felt regarding drinking. I said that I didn't like hangovers; I said that I didn't like drinking each night; I said that I worried about all the rules that I would make for myself and break.

She said that those were good reasons, but I needed to go deeper on the issues of why I just stopped. I started crying and said: *I just did.*

I'm upset. I am feeling so anxious. I was so excited because she seemed like she was totally going to support me.

I'm not going to drink . . . but I felt stupid in the therapy session, and I couldn't think of what to say, and I wanted to leave, and isn't not drinking a control issue for everyone? I mean if I say I'm not drinking, I'm controlling that. Ugggghhh.

Also, I was talking to my husband, and again, he said: 'I'm not going to say anything, but I'm still not sure where you're going with this, but I want you to be happy.' Then, he cracked open a beer."

me: Yeah, maybe this therapist isn't for you, and that's fine, there are lots of therapists in the world. You want someone who understands what we're doing. Those of us online are probably drinking more? Where does that even come from? That's not an informed comment, clearly. Drinking more than people in AA? I don't think so :)

It's OK. If you were trying to find a 'dentist' and if the dentist made you cry then you wouldn't go back to them and you'd find another dentist who gets it.

What a shitty thing for her to do. Really. She's not validating what you're saying you want. Like really, we all need to be drinking? Like no one can decide not to drink and be happy about it? Oh god.

If you want to talk to ME (ha!) I have one spot open on Friday. Let me know. Love, me

WHAT SOBER MEMOIRS DO YOU RECOMMEND?

I have not had very good luck reading the alcohol-women-recovery books. In addition to not associating with the low-bottom stories, I find that alcohol memoirs tend to romanticize drinking, all the talk of deep reds and crisp notes of buttery blah-blah. Long descriptions of drinking sessions tend to make me feel like drinking. No shit. You know what I'm talking about!

And really, I don't need to read about how bad it was (she drank, fell down, she drank again, she fell down again). I always ended up comparing myself to the *depths of hell* presented in the text, and would find my situation to be "not as bad as theirs," and thus I could convince myself that I didn't have a problem and that it was OK for me to keep drinking.

> **from M:** "That's the trouble with the drunkalogues. I know how everyone gets in. I like to hear about how people have gotten the fuck out."

I think we read sober books looking for a connection, searching for shared stories so that we can feel less alone. But it can be false company if a disproportionate number of pages in the book are spent on drinking stories, compared to the weight given to recovery and how to go forward in the sober world.

How about, instead, we focus on tools, strategies, and how-to. How about we find ways to relate and connect with the *success* stories. My advice is to read carefully. If you begin reading and it makes you feel weird, then you can stop. Find texts that support you. There are many people writing sober blogs, and a lot of them have success stories. For example, I know one you can begin with. (Mine!)

That said, I loved "Dry," by Augusten Burroughs. I read and liked Jason Vale's "Kick the Drink Easily" (with some reservations; I don't agree with his ideas on when to quit, or whether to count days—see below).

DO I HAVE TO COUNT DAYS?

> **from Clementine:** "Why do you think it's important to have continuous sober time? Why is it more valuable to have 60 days in a row, than to have 29 days, a week off drinking, and then 29 more days (like me)?"

I think day counting is important because each day represents a day when you said NO. You are building a wall between the 'you' back there, and the 'new you' over here, and so every sober day is a new brick in that wall.

There are many forums and online communities that have pledges like "let's plan to do 15 out of 30 days sober this month," but they are not continuous days.

This doesn't help us; we don't get anywhere. On the days we're not drinking, we are waiting to drink again. It's like holding your breath and going underwater for a day.

To me, the reason for a longer goal (100 days) is that you have to actually go forward and learn something. Once you remove the booze, you practise new things like self-soothing, treats, and learning to change the channel in your head.

If you don't pay attention to your sober momentum, then *any* day can be a drinking day or a sober day. By counting, you're saying to Wolfie: "I'm not doing this. I'm getting the hell out of here. As far as I can, far away from you. One sober day at a time."

~~~~~~~~~~

Resource:
Audio ~ Sober Podcast 109. Continuous Days Sober, www.100daysoberchallenge.com/SP109

WHAT DOES RELAPSE MEAN?

from Alison: "Please reset me again on Day 1."

People sometimes have relapses and I get emails from penpals asking me to restart their day count. Alison from the quote above had had several restarts, so I was worried that she didn't have enough supports.

If you and me (and Alison) put together our own sobriety programs as some kind of jigsaw puzzle, then each person needs a different configuration. Your version of sober support might include reading sober blogs but not writing comments. Another person's toolkit might include writing a blog and commenting on others. Some go to AA. Others go to AA and read and write blogs and listen to sober audios.

There is no one solution. I know that makes it seem complicated. "Thanks Belle, how am I supposed to know what will work for me?"

If you're like me, you start with a few sober tools that resonate with you. Usually easy ones. And if you hate being sober, find it to be a real struggle, feel like you're white-knuckling, or if you relapse, then you know that you need to add more tools.

If you are Alison, and have repeated Day 1s after not very much momentum, then I will say: "Have you thought about what else you can add? What you're doing now is good, but it's not quite enough. You perhaps have the right supports and tools to get you started, but not enough to keep you going. Do you know what you could add?"

When I asked Alison this question, she replied: "I have lots of support. My husband and my mother-in-law have been fabulous."

I read that email before bed. And all night, literally, all I could think of was what I wanted to say to her: "Having those two people is fabulous, but it's not enough. If you had enough in the way of tools and supports, you would be continuously sober. And you're not. So it's not enough."

(I recorded a sober podcast addressing Alison's specific email, trying to better explain the idea of Not Quite Enough. You'll see the link to the podcast in the resources box at the end of this section.)

When Alison says *I have good support*, my heart breaks for her. Because she does have something that lots of us don't have: two, in-real-life cheerleaders who think she's fabulous, who are on her side, who she can tell when she's struggling.

When I quit drinking I didn't have anybody in real life that I could talk to, so the fact that she has these two support people? That's a big deal.

But in her case it's not enough. And despite what she may say, I KNOW it's not enough because she's not continuously sober.

I think it's easy to confuse "sober support and tools" with having a mother-in-law or a husband. Sober support is anything—person, tool, or strategy—that makes it easier for you to not drink.

For example, you can order take-out, go to bed early, have sober treats, have accountability, speak to your doctor about medication, practise meditation, swim, go running, make yourself a bitter drink, have a sober coach—these are all sober supports.*

---

* I challenged myself to write out 60 different sober tools and supports, from 'go to bed early' all the way to 'inpatient rehab' and my list is in the Appendix.

You'll read this list of suggested supports and you'll say "that's very nice, Belle, but I can't add *order take-out* to my list of tools, and expect it to help keep me from drinking."

Yes, you can.

You can, because it's one way of reducing overwhelm.

If we have a bizarre, unfortunate, unforgiving, and heinous combination of a lack of self-soothing techniques, a sensitive disposition, a tendency to be overwhelmed, and a stubborn pride, then yes, giving up making dinner for the first several weeks of being sober CAN help. Of course it can. *Because it all can help.*

---

from sophiesomething (day 260): "I didn't really cook dinner for 6 months. Just couldn't face cooking and not drinking. My husband ate a lot of rolled up cold cuts . . . Now I can cook again. Love cooking again. Took longer than I'd have thought. But not a problem, wine-wise."

You don't know which tools are going to work. So you're going to try all of them.

We can dissect other sober tools in the same way: "Belle, I'm finding it very hard to stay sober, I need more sober tools, but I don't think listening to audios will be enough to help me."

Listening to audios won't be the ONLY tool you'll need, but it can be one of them. Here's what happens when you listen to an audio: You have a one-on-one experience with the person speaking. The human voice can be very calming and audio has a way of going right into your head and helping you 'think' differently. You will find part of an audio that makes you feel hopeful, and replay it over and over. Isn't that what prayer is? Repetition of comforting words that make us feel uplifted and connected?

---

from Tekara: "Your recordings do help a lot. Thanks for making them, and for choosing to help people through humour. Thinking about alcohol can be so heavy, that it's nice to laugh about the shittiness of what it does as we plot our course to be free."

OK, so here's the thing to remember. If you've been trying to get some sober momentum and it's not working, then add more tools, more supports, more things. Try different.

~~~~~~~~~~

Resources:

Audio ~ Sober Podcast 079: Not Quite Enough,
www.100daysoberchallenge.com/SP079

Audio ~ One Minute Message 040: What Does Relapse Mean?
www.100daysoberchallenge.com/relapseaudio

HOW CAN I SEE A RELAPSE BEFORE IT HAPPENS?

> **from Cass (Day 3):** "Hi Belle wish I could say 'all good, cruising along booze-free', but unfortunately that's not the case. I don't know what happened . . . I was feeling OK, not missing drinking except for the occasional passing moment but nothing too intense and then BAM! Wolfie came out of nowhere with such force and wore me down so here I am feeling pretty frustrated, disappointed, and a little puzzled by what happened the other night."

The period of time *before* people drink is what I call 'pre-lapse' which maybe isn't a word, but it is now. Prelapse is the time before relapse.

At first, when I ask a penpal what was happening *before* their relapse, they don't know. But if we rewind the tape, and go back over the two or three days previous, usually we can find *prelapse*: an emotional state where our brain says 'fuck it'. Like, "I'm overwhelmed with work, this is all too much, it's all too hard." That doesn't sound like Wolfie. It doesn't sound like "you should drink right now." But it can lead to the same place.

Whenever you hear "This is all too hard" or "This isn't worth it," then consider the voice in your head to be a big red warning sign that prelapse is on the horizon.

Your feelings of overwhelm may not specifically be about drinking. Perhaps it's the never-ending mountain of laundry, or the dog vomiting, or that you haven't planned dinner yet.

It could be that you haven't had enough sleep, and you start to feel like "this isn't worth it." But you go to bed early, and the next day is fine, so you're not in prelapse anymore.

Sometimes we get that "this is all too hard" feeling when we're sick, or when our children are sick, but when we are feeling better it stops.

If you are in prelapse, then you will want to do things right away that might make you feel better. Even if you have to try things mechanically, one after the other. You'll say "I got enough sleep that didn't work, had a nap that didn't work, went for a run that didn't work." Then you go on to the next thing. You have a treat, that didn't work. You watch bad TV, that didn't work. You read blogs, write in your journal, comment on blogs, listen to audios, email somebody, reach out, go to a meeting, listen to something inspirational—you go through the toolkit.

And here's something that will seem obvious when I say it: If the first tool doesn't work, it does not mean that the whole thing is hopeless. It means that you go on to the next tool.

~~~~~~~~~

Resource:

Audio ~ Sober Podcast 046: Prelapse,
www.100daysoberchallenge.com/prelapse

IS IT ME OR IS IT WOLFIE?

Wolfie is the booze voice, the noise in your head that tries to make drinking seem like a good idea. In the beginning, it's hard to sort out all of the noise and identify the thinking that is Wolfie, and the ideas that are really from you. Wolfie can sound rational and convincing but with a bit of practise, you'll be able to tell them apart. Here's a primer.

Wolfie: OK maybe I wasn't ready to go to a pub, but it's unrealistic to think that I can't go out with my friends, I mean I'm 24 and I live in Los Angeles.

You: I wasn't ready, I put myself in a tempting place, I have to be more careful and vigilant and not do that again until I'm much further along, if ever.

W: I had a drink but honestly it has been building for days and I just wanted the noise in my head to stop.

You: I had a drink and then another. I didn't realize that I was in prelapse beforehand. Next time I will reach out, sleep, cry, have chocolate, meditate, run, and email my penpal until something works. It's not that there are no tools, it's that I don't have the right combination yet.

W: I drank yesterday but I don't think it counts because I only had one glass and I made it last for a long time and I didn't get drunk, so I can still say 'sober' for yesterday.

You: I drank yesterday. Today is Day 1.

W: I don't want to count days. It makes me tense.

You: As much as I resist it, I know that I will count days (at least to begin). Each day represents a solid, discrete length of time when I said NO to alcohol. The days add up, the wall between me and my Day 1 gets stronger. Momentum is important.

W: I don't want treats. They makes me tense.

You: I guess I've never thought about treats. But my reward system is screwed up, that's for sure. My brain thinks that alcohol is the reward for everything. For anything. I have to relearn other kinds of treats even if it feels awkward at first.

W: I don't want to do anything different this time. It's all fine. I don't want to add any other supports. No thank you to an audio or a call or to reaching out. I just have to try harder.

You: I want to do something different this time. I do OK for a while and then I lose the plot. I will add some tools/supports that I haven't tried before.

W: Oh I'm so tired of myself, I'm never going to figure this out.

You: Oh I'm so tired of myself, I *have* to figure this out, because I want to be done with this. I do not want a new Day 1.

DON'T I JUST NEED TO TRY HARDER?

> **from Nost:** "I feel like a loser. Like I just fail all the time and I don't know why. Maybe I just have to try harder. I don't know what else to do."

There are a lot of us who come to quitting drinking with a 'try harder' attitude like Nost has. "I'll begin tomorrow, and I'll try harder."

Think about weight loss instead of drinking. Let's say I am trying to lose weight, and every day I start with good intentions, and maybe I do well for a few days, but then I eat a piece of cake. A few days later I eat an entire cake. I start the diet again with: "I just have to try harder."

How about instead of trying harder, I tried *different*?

Different things I could do: remove the cake from the house, remove all of the junk or processed food from the house—give it away, donate to the women's shelter, throw it out. (Remove the alcohol, give it away, donate to friends at work, pour it out.)

I could go to the store and get healthy food for an entire week, plan all seven days' worth of meals, throw in a few snacks, and a few healthy treats like raisins and pineapple. (Get sober replacement drinks, lots of different kinds, and teas and decaf coffee, and some sober reward treats like raisins and pineapple.)

I'd tell someone that I'm starting a new eating thing and ask for their support. (I could have a sober penpal and a place where I can be accountable.)

I could find a blog written by someone who has successfully changed their eating and read their blog from day one to see what they struggled with and how they coped. (Hey, I know a good sobriety blog!)

I can have an appointment with a food person. (I could have a call with a sober coach, a counsellor, a therapist.)

I can subscribe to a podcast about healthy eating. (Hey I know a good sober podcast series!)

Or I can try harder. I can get up tomorrow, with all of the booze still in my house, with all the same stress as yesterday, with the court case and the in-laws and the car brakes and the snow and the vacation and the fundraiser and the laundry and the special needs child, and I can say that starting today I'm going to "try harder."

If you've been trying things to be sober, you can say this to yourself: "I'm going to quit for 100 days even if I hate it. I want to see how much better being sober is, Belle assures me it's worth it."

And it is.

Now that I've convinced you to 'try different', you're thinking: *What can I do that's different. I don't feel like anything is going to work.* Keep reading. You'll like the next section. And don't forget that there's a list of 60 Sober Tools in the Appendix.

ARE THERE RULES TO FOLLOW TO BE SUCCESSFUL?

---

from L: "Is there a set of rules that I can follow that will help me be sober? I'd like a checklist. I'm a good student!"

There is no secret handshake and there is no checklist. But I can say that after emailing a squillion people, I have seen some patterns that indicate if you're more likely to be successful.

Can you do these things? Do as many as you can.

You are more likely to be successful if you:

- Reach out for support. It's hard. Do it anyway.
- Sign up to have a sober penpal. Email your penpal every day.
- Share real stuff, don't exaggerate, and don't leave things out. Be truly honest with at least one person in your life about your booze stuff.
- Reach out instead of drink, cry instead of drink, walk instead, email me frustrated instead (the people who don't email are more likely to get alone in their head with Wolfie who will always say that drinking is a good idea).
- Remember that successful treaters do MUCH better. It's shocking how much better they do. Once you figure out the self-care treat thing, you'll find this whole sober experience to be much easier. If you resist treats, don't understand them, don't think they apply to you, then I worry about you (see below).
- Get enough support, load on a lot to begin and then ease off as time goes by and you feel stable. Be cautious. Don't fuck with sober momentum.
- Tell on Wolfie—share when you're having weird thoughts, externalize the voice, tell on your inner addict.
- Read stuff that supports you and turn away from what doesn't. You don't read about moderation, you don't read blogs that get under your skin, you turn away from people who repeatedly relapse if that makes you feel wobbly.

- Protect your sobriety, avoid situations and people that may trigger you. Your sobriety is a like a little chick that can easily get squished in traffic.

Things that make me worry about you:

On the other hand, when I see you doing some of these things below, then I worry. So let me come through the page, right now, and say this directly to you: I will worry about you if you do any of this:

- If you drift from your supports that have been working for you, because you don't think you need them anymore.
- If you are disagreeable about the idea of treats, or support, or the 'name' of Wolfie, nitpicking the details . . . and you're on Day 0.
- If you tell me you're *certain* that you need to figure out why you drink, think your way through it, before you can be sober.
- If you prioritize weight loss over sobriety.
- If you hang out in online sober forums and chat rooms where repeated relapsing is normal, and if not overtly encouraged, it is met with an implicit permission of "that's OK, just try again tomorrow."
- If you sip from the straw of support, taking small sips here and there, instead of loading on big gulps (how's that for mixing metaphors).
- If you insist that supports come from one place instead of another. It may not come from your spouse. If you say you don't have enough support,

then maybe you've been looking in the wrong places.

- If you repeatedly feel the need to be brave and test yourself, putting yourself in tempting situations too early just to *see what happens*. Or you tell me "I can't hide at home forever, you know." This shit worries me.

- If you try to do too much at once.

- If you change your medication without medical advice.

- If you delete your email address.

- If you have relapsed ten times, and I kindly suggest that you remove the alcohol from your home, and you don't, then I worry about you. I don't have all the answers. No one does. But I am sober. And you're on Day 0. So you could remove the booze from your home, just for kicks, to see if it helps.

- If you are overly frustrated with your 'slow' progress then I will worry about you. Here's the question: Are you sober? Then you're doing fine for now. Being sober is a big deal and is worth celebrating. Sober first. Everything else second.

~~~~~~~~~

Resources:

Audio ~ Sober Podcast 018: Chicken Little,
www.100daysoberchallenge.com/SP018

Audio ~ Sober Podcast 019: Little Chick in the Grass,
www.100daysoberchallenge.com/SP019

Audio ~ Sober Podcast 022: I Heart Chicks,
www.100daysoberchallenge.com/SP022

Blog post ~ Then we take on the world (about weight loss),
www.100daysoberchallenge.com/weightloss

APPENDIX:
60 MAGIC SOBER TOOLS

YOU CAN BEGIN by picking 10 things from this list, sober tools you can begin to implement this week. Better yet, don't fuck around, pick 30 things and load on the support. You can always ease off later once you have some sober momentum.

1. Write in a journal every day for your first 30 days sober, no matter what (can be private, or anonymous on a blog, doesn't matter).

2. Read sober blogs at least one hour a day, every day. I was reading for one to two hours a day for the first 60 days. Find blogs that support you. Read the occasional "New Day 1" story to remind you to stay away from Day 1 and keep moving forward. Even if the way forward seems unclear and foggy.

3. Rethink your evening routine and give up making dinner if it's too much. You can make meals in the morning to reheat, or have easier dinners (pasta and jarred sauce), or take-out, or delegate.

4. Have a bath/shower every evening, early, so that it sets the mood for the rest of the night. Maybe bath first and then dinner.

5. Plan and purchase replacement drinks that you can have during the witching hours. Bitter is better.

6. Have a version of the story that you can tell as to why you're not drinking. You may have different stories depending on who you're talking to. Plan in advance what you might say.

7. Change your schedule for when you eat dinner (earlier/later). If you have to feed kids or others earlier, fine, but you can eat at different times— for a month. Schedule something to coincide with Wolfie time (like feed kids and then listen to an audio in the tub for half an hour). Or go to the gym right at 7 p.m. and eat later. Change your routine so that you are not operating on autopilot.

8. Remove the alcohol from your home. Pour it out, move it to a friend's house, give it away.

9. Get yourself daily treats for the first two weeks, and then something every two days thereafter. For as long as you want.

10. Plan your Day 30, Day 60, Day 90 and Day 100 treats in advance. Go online now and put them in your shopping cart.

11. Get as much sleep as humanly possible. Take naps. You will need a lot more sleep than you anticipate.

12. Go to bed every time you feel crappy, when you feel you're about to drink, or when you are agitated and need a time-out. Bed is a good, safe place to hide.

13. Give up any expectations that you're going to 'get stuff done' and just be sober. Being sober is

enough. Sober first. If you push yourself too hard, and load on too many goals at once, Wolfie comes in with "this is all too hard."

14. Pretend, for a while, that you're sick, that you have the flu, that you need to take good care of you—very, very good care. Pretend that you come first. Just for now.

15. Try to do some kind of physical exercise every day, even if it's only for 10 minutes and you have to drag the kids along with you. The more exercise the better, but even walking is good. Head out your front door for five minutes, then turn around and walk home. Don't make it any more complicated than that.

16. Rent/stream new TV shows and movies as your sober treats, that you can watch only if sober. Have you seen *Transparent*? It's genius. Also check out *Six Feet Under, Breaking Bad, Better Call Saul* and the *Great British Bake-off. Downton Abbey* is pretty good, too. So is *Catastrophe*.

17. Give up doing the laundry so often.

18. Give up any ideas of a clean and tidy house for now.

19. Talk to your doctor about medication, like maybe anti-booze medication (antabuse), or anti-depressants or anti-anxiety or whatever might help. If you don't think you can honestly speak with your current doctor about your drinking, then go to a clinic and talk to someone else. If you've tried seeing your family doctor and you're not happy with

the medication or the dosage, then get a referral for a visit to a psychiatrist. They're the experts when it comes to treating our brains.

20. Please know that crying is totally normal, required, and necessary. Your guts will feel like they're raw and on the outside of your body. This will feel both great and exciting AND unreal and scary. Crying is normal.

21. Sign up for a free daily sober audio. You don't know of any? No problem: Belle's One Minute (sober) Message ~ **www.sobermessage.com/signup**

22. If you are a Sober Jumpstart student and have been assigned a sober penpal, then email every day, to check in on how you're feeling.

23. Think about what you're going to GET by being sober. The benefits coming to you. How great it'll be once the first crappy part is over (see more in Section 13: Focus on what you get).

24. Take pictures of things that you're grateful for now that you're sober. It can be simple things like a good cup of coffee, the view from the window, your girls playing dress-up. You can do a sober photo project. It can last 16 days, or 100 days.

25. Avoid overwhelm as much as possible. In fact, strive for "underwhelm" and engage in some truly slothful behaviours. It's OK to be in your jammies watching a show on your iPad. You're sober. Sometimes bed-snuggle time is required.

26. Pet your cat, dog, or horse. You know already that this makes you feel better.

27. Decline most social invitations that involve alcohol for the first 4-6 weeks. Really, it takes some time to feel less wobbly about socializing. The general rule is if you feel weird, don't go. You do NOT have to push yourself to "act like normal." Your job is to be sober. Meet people for lunch. Go bowling. Skip pubs. Skip sporting events that are mainly an excuse to drink. It's not permanent; later, you'll be able to attend these sorts of events, but to begin you won't.

28. For the social gatherings that you DO attend, you can arrive late, leave early, bring your own replacement drink, and say that you have something else to go to afterwards as you walk out 60 minutes after you've arrived.

29. Listen to sober audio and podcasts (mine or others). Find specific topics or episodes that resonate with you. Listen to them on repeat.

30. Accept that sober motivation is like deodorant: it needs to be reapplied every day. Stop feeling like you should be able to do this if you 'try harder'. You will need to 'try different'.

31. Ask for help.

32. Accept help. Let other people do things for you.

33. Ask for and listen to advice from other successfully sober people.

34. Go to a face-to-face meeting (even once a week would be helpful). You can go to AA. You can go to a Recovery Ring meeting. You can go to NA. You

can go to Al-Anon. You can sit in the room and not speak, just listen.

35. Another tool? Have a sponsor.

36. Work the steps.

37. Share at meetings.

38. Speak to your doctor about part-time outpatient treatment through your local hospital that you can attend on evenings or weekends.

39. Ask about full-time outpatient treatment.

40. Ask about in-patient treatment (rehab).

41. Ask about sober living, extended places where you can live sober.

42. Tell who you want, what you want, when you want to. Be relieved to discover that most people won't care if we're drinking or not. Only a boozer with a loud Wolfie would give you a hard time.

43. See irritating people as people with struggles. We were irritating too. We were dealing with stuff that other people couldn't see. Drop your shoulders and see that woman as lonely, or hurt, or needy. She's not trying intentionally to make you crazy.

44. Share the nonsensical things that Wolfie tells you—share with another sober person who will truly 'get it'. Be shocked and then amused that we all hear virtually the same thing.

45. Find some small activities to do in the evenings to help occupy the empty time. It doesn't take long for regular life to flow back into the spaces that alcohol consumed, but to begin it's helpful to have

some projects. If you need one, there's the cupcake exercise. Make and photograph each of these recipes: **www.100daysoberchallenge.com/cupcake**

46. Decluttering is helpful. It's cleaning up, from the outside in. Yes I've made an audio for this.

47. Have something you can wear, some special piece of jewelry, that reminds you that you're sober and that you're special. Rub the jewelry. Bestow it with super powers. You can start with the 'Fuck You Wolfie' bracelet and go from there. (I'm sorry, I'm not trying—repeatedly—to sell you stuff. All the things in my sober store are items I have created because I needed them, like I truly needed my FUW bracelet. It saved my ass plenty of times.)

48. Go to sober meetups in random cities either with groups that I set up, or ones you arrange through other online forums. Meeting other people is eye-opening. You are not alone. Not at all. And all those other people? They look 'normal'.

49. If you have to travel for work, speak to your employer and let them know that you would like to travel less if possible, and that if you do travel, you'd like to (a) have your own transportation so that you can leave events when you're ready, (b) stay in hotels without bars or (c) ask for mini-bars to be emptied before you arrive, and (d) fly coach.

50. Accept that there is no weight loss in early sobriety and give up any ideas of radically changing your diet or training for an Ironman and doing early

sobriety at the same time. Sober first. Everything else hinges on you being sober. Sober first. Everything else second. Did you hear me? Sober first.

51. Find ONE person that you can be 100% honest with about your drinking, about your thinking, your worries, your struggles, your excitement, and your joy. That might be a counsellor, sober mentor, a coach, sponsor, or a sober friend. You should have at least ONE person who truly gets what it's like to be you.

52. Accept that the first time you do everything, it's going to be a little weird. The first weekend is weird. The first time going for sushi is weird. The first sober sex, the first flight, the first sober vacation. And then sober becomes the new normal.

53. When you are facing a shitty hard thing, or a weirdly tempting event (like a staff party), then plan a sober treat you'll have AFTER you're home again, safe and sober. Don't skip this step. Wolfie likes to come in with "where's my reward" after we do something hard. So you want to remember to have these treats pre-planned. Like, if you go on vacation, find it tough, and then get home and wonder why you feel so weird and let down . . . then get a treat. Do it right now. See the blog for my story of the wedding catering + the ice cream cone.

54. Be pretty darn proud of yourself. Being sober is a big deal, and this is you doing it. You being proud

of you, being able to count on yourself, is a huge big deal. It's gigantic. It's nearly the best part of being sober. You have to celebrate your successes. No one is coming in to do this for you. It's you. It's up to you.

55. When attending family events with people you don't like, then you can do the dishes, talk with the teenagers, sit on the floor with the kids, go outside for a break, email from the bathroom, and play dysfunctional family bingo.

56. Walk out of your office, cross the street, have a cry, get a take-out coffee and a pastry, call it a sober treat, email me that you're doing OK, and then go back to work. Even if you remove yourself 'briefly' from whatever situation is making you feel crazy, you can give yourself some time to settle and feel better.

57. If you relapse (once, or more than once) OR you are sober but feeling shitty, then add more sober tools from this list. I know this is a bit meta, but this sober tool is: Add more tools.

58. Probably 50% of my penpals have an underlying issue with anxiety or depression that doesn't immediately go away when they're sober. If you haven't tried medication or therapy when sober, you might want to revisit the idea of both. Me personally, I want to redo ALL of my therapy now that I'm sober. I'm sure it'd be a lot more efficient and useful. And there'd be a lot less lying.

59. Find tools that work and keep using them. Don't drift from your sober supports. Read this book again. Listen to the audios again. Keep your hands on 10-and-2. You know how people stop taking their blood pressure medication as soon as they feel better? What if feeling better was the goal? How about you keep doing whatever's working. I get emails all the time that say "I'm on day 80 and I'm feeling good, do you think I can just listen to audios once a week instead of once a day? (Or can I stop going to meetings, or do you think it would be smart for me to stop doing tool XYZ?)" And my answer will always be the same. Whatever you're doing is working, so keep doing it. Know that Wolfie wants to get us alone in our head, where he can say: *"Drinking seems like a good idea. You can probably have one."* Resist this kind of wolfie-solo-nonsense-manipulation by reaching out, telling on your inner addict. Wolfie is a bully and hates it when we share.

60. It's possible that one of these tools will be magic for you. It's also possible, and more likely, that any individual sober tool contributes only 5% towards your success, but you don't know which tools are the key ones. So you do a bunch of them. Because having a new Day 1 sucks rocks, and once you have sober momentum you don't fuck with it.

THE END (FOR NOW)

HERE ARE SOME PARTING WORDS.

You can quit drinking without telling everyone you have a PROBLEM. You don't even have to tell your spouse to begin. You will find a way of explaining what you're doing that feels right for you.

It's entirely possible to quit drinking if your partner works in a brewery, or if they drink the contents of a brewery, or if they think that online sober support is a scam/cult. Yes, what you're doing is for YOU. Your partner is on their own road. You can do what's best for you.

Your kids do notice when you're drinking, and yes they notice when you stop. They notice in ways that they'll never be able to explain with words. Because something like 'trust' doesn't have easy language to describe it. Your children notice. They will not use words to tell you how they notice.

You will feel gigantically shitty if you drink for two days, are sober for one or two days, drink again for five days, and then quit again. It's true that hanging around Day 1 is the hardest place to be. It's harder than being sober. Day 1 is too close to the sewer. It's time to step out into the light.

Yes, repeatedly relapsing does mean something. It means that whatever you're doing so far is good, but it's not enough. You need to add more supports. If each time you restart you add more supports, then your sober toolkit is more likely to help you get and keep sober momentum. Sometimes the support you need will be rehab. Sometimes the support you will need is more connection with other sober humans. Sometimes the support you need will be AA. Sometimes the support you need will be listening to sober podcasts. It's not about 'trying harder'. Relapse means: What else can you add?

I do believe you can do it, even when you don't believe it yet. I have been on Day 1 and Day 7 and day 37 and Day 287. I felt like there were two versions of me: the 'real' version of me that was a drinker, and a new 'shadow' sober version of me, walking alongside. It took a LONG time until I felt that the new sober me was the 'real' me. Thankfully, while I was going along, *it didn't matter.* I kept doing the sober thing until the fake drinking me faded entirely. That you can see both versions doesn't mean you're doing anything wrong. Keep going.

---

from AG (day 298): "The further away I get from Day 1, the more I'm amazed that I used to think I 'deserved' alcohol. What a cancer of the mind that Wolfie is! . . . I pray now for the newly sober—that they can just hold on long enough to get on this side of things. They only need to do two things: don't drink, and trust in EVERYTHING you say. Just those two things can transform a life!"

I know this sounds like proselytizing, but I didn't pay her to write this. I have an inbox full of messages like this. I look forward to seeing one from you :)

love, Belle
xo

Paris, February 26, 2016

All of the quotes in this book are from real sober people, and were either received by email or posted as comments on my blog.

You're still here :) That's good.

If you've enjoyed this book (hooray), you might like the **PDF/Kindle version** which includes *extra* things that I couldn't fit into the print edition because of length. The e-book version includes my recipe for Banana Bread. And the one for Tiramisu (made without alcohol). And the divine recipe for Fuck You Wolfie Lemonade.

www.100daysoberchallenge.com/electronicversion

If you've enjoyed this book (yippee), you might like the **audio** version. Yes, there is a big long audio of me reading 100% of this text (not abridged, the whole thing). And yes, there are different bits in the audio that aren't in either the print or electronic versions. Sometimes when recording the book text, I'd have a new idea or an aside, and so I shared those too. Also the audio version includes embedded One Minute Message audios as well as a bonus full-length podcast episode.

www.100daysoberchallenge.com/audioversion

About the Author

Belle Robertson, born in Canada, is a bossy older sister in her late 40s (sigh), and lives in Paris with her French-speaking husband (who is also Canadian). She is kidless and dogless.

Educated at St. Mary's University (Bachelor of Arts), and the University of British Columbia (Bachelor of Education, Master of Fine Arts in Creative Writing), she works as a text designer, baker & caterer, and as a sober coach. She types 130 words a minute. She is a fan of parentheses. She appreciates the fine art of swearing. She continues to search for the perfect lemon doughnut.

About the Author